APARTHEID

AN ILLUSTRATED HISTORY

APARTHEID

AN ILLUSTRATED HISTORY

MICHAEL MORRIS

JONATHAN BALL PUBLISHERS
Johannesburg & Cape Town

THE SABOTAGE TRIALISTS

South Africa enters 1964 with the world watching more closely than ever before. The centre of world interest is focussed on the Sabotage Trials throughout the land, at which some of the country's top political leaders face charges that could mean their lives. Here DRUM gives pen pictures of the men involved in the three main cases.

TRANSVAAL

Walter Sisulu, ex-secretary general of ANC. Treason Trialist. Disappeared early this year. Was among those arrested in the Rivonia Raid.

Raymond Mhlaba, of Port Elizabeth. A local ANC leader, prominent in Defiance Campaign. Official of Sactu. Disappeared in 1962: arrested at Rivonia

Nelson Mandela. Treason Trialist. Was jailed in '62 for six years. One of best known ex-ANC officials. Was legal partner of Oliver Tambo.

Lionel 'Rusty' Bernstein. Ex-member Congress of Democrats. A Johannesburg architect. Also arrested during Rivonia Raid.

Dennis Goldberg, leading member of the Congress of Democrats in Cape. Civil engineer. Noted as public speaker. Arrested in Rivonia Raid.

Ahmed Kathrada, Treason Trialist. Ex-sec. Ind. Youth League. Went underground during house arrest. Was picked up in Rivonia Raid.

James Kantor. Top criminal lawyer. Acted for several political leaders. Brother-in-law of Harold Wolpe, who escaped from jail.

Andrew Mlangeni and Elias Motsoaledi, the two 'mystery men' of the Rivonia trial. Both active in the ANC in Johannesburg, figured in the Defiance Campaign and both detained during the 1960 Emergency. Mlangeni also active in Dube Advisory Board elections. Both charged with the others but not listed under High Command.

Govan Mbeki, top ANC man in East Cape. Journalist, one-time teacher. Treason Trialist. Held in Emergency. Disappeared before arrest at Rivonia.

NATAL

Billy Nair, 34. Trade unionist. Secretary of SACTU since 1955. Jailed for part in 1952 Defiance Campaign. Treason Trialist. Detained during 1960 State of Emergency.

Ebrahim Ismail, 25. Joined Nat. Ind. Con. in 1952. Delegate to Kliptown Congress of People in 1955. After matric, worked as a reporter on New Age. Detained in August.

Sunny Singh, 24. Joined Nat. Ind. Youth Con. 1961 and became member Nat. Ind. Con. 1962. Was a part-time student and salesman at time of arrest in August.

Kisten Moonsamy, 29. Org. Sec. of Clairwood South branch, Nat. Ind. Con. Re-organised Sweet Workers' Industrial Union. Active in sport.

CURNICK NDLOVU. Trade unionist and active in ANC as a Youth Leguer until 1960 ban. Confined to Durban and Kwa Mashu for five yrs. Detained under 90-day law in June.

Kisten Doorsamy, 29. Joined Nat. Ind. Con. in '60. Once charged for taking part in a placard demonstration. Family's sole support. Detained in July.

Ragavan Kistensamy, 24. Chairman Nat. Ind. Con. Sweet Workers' Union. Engaged before arrest. Keen on sport

Natvarlal Babenia, 39. Worked in Nat. Ind. Congress as a clerk. Campaigned in India under Mahatma Gandhi. Returned in '49. Was an editor of Indian Opinion, paper founded by Gandhi.

Riot Mhkwanazi. A New Age seller until banning in 1963. Detained in 1960 emergency. Was member of African Textile Workers' Union.

Alfred Duma, 33. Ardent trade unionist and former member ANC. Was chairman of 'Umviko Party of Besters. Is married with 3 children.

Shadrack Maphumulo, 25. Active as trade unionist. Member of General Workers' Union in 1961. Employed in a bank at the time of his detention.

Matthews Meyiwa, 39. Rose to top post in chemical factory in few years. Also high official in Congregational Church. Vice-chairman of Georgedale Landowners' Ass: Detained in June

Bernard Nkosi, 41. Comes from Georgedale district. Sec. of Metal Workers' Union since 1961. Before arrest was employed by same firm for 22 years.

GEORGE NAICKER, Member Nat. Ind. Con. since 1944. Leader of S.A. delegation to the World Fed. of Democratic Youth Festival in Moscow, 1957. Was detained in '60 emergency.

Zakhele Mdlalose, 38. Another trialist from Georgedale area. Was a member of ANC. Before arrest, was employed by Durban shoe shop 10 years.

David Mhkize, 35. Home is in New Hanover District. Member of ANC and General Workers' Union since 1958. Is married and has five sons.

David Ndawonde, 31. Chairman of African Tea and Coffee Workers' Union. Was sec. Somtseu ANC branch until it was banned. Worked at Durban tea factory until his detention.

Joshua Zulu, 39. Principal Albert Falls Govt. School for past six years. Preacher in Anglican Church. Active in teaching affairs. Detained in July.

Siva Pillay, 20. Was member Natal Indian Youth Con. since 1961. Was detained at Salisbury Univ. College, where he was B.Sc. student, in August.

CAPE

The Reverend Don Davis. He is 42 and one of the best-known and most popular preachers in the Peninsula. He is the eldest of the eleven people standing trial in the Cape.

Neville Alexander, doctor of philosophy. Took his degree in Germany. Professors and students there have started a fund for his defence.

Elizabeth van den Heyden. Teacher, B.A. graduate. It is alleged that she visited Dr. Ken Abrahams in S.W. Africa before his flight

Ian Leslie van den Heyden. Detained in July with Dr Alexander, he was released and then re-detained. A graduate teacher at Livingstone.

Doris van den Heyden, sister to Ian and Elizabeth van den Heyden. She holds a university degree and worked as a librarian when held.

Marcus Solomons, 23. Was teaching at Walmer Estate Primary School before his arrest in Jo'burg. Is ex-Hewat College student.

Dulcie September, popular teacher at Silvertown, standing trial with fellow teachers. Unmarried. Arrested and held in September.

Fikili Bam, 26-year-old student at Cape Town University. Studying law. Arrested in Johannesburg with Marcus Solomons. He is a bachelor.

Gordon Frederick Hendricks, the young Cape intellectual who, with ten others, is charged with setting up a 'Chinese Poqo' group

Lionel Davis, 26-year-old bachelor. Lived with his mother. A clerk. Detained in Cape Town in September. He was known to like twist parties.

Contents

Front cover
Modderdam 'squatter camp' residents flee a cloud of tear gas during a 1977 police raid.

Pages 2-3
The writing was on the wall for apartheid rule by the mid-1980s, when demands for the freeing of leaders like Nelson Mandela, deftly drawn in this contemporary graffiti in Woodstock, Cape Town, became irrepressible.

Pages 4-5
Township patrols by the security forces invariably stimulated the resistance that the security establishment counted on its soldiers to quell.

Opposite page
'Sabotage trials' in the 1960s earned South Africa lasting notoriety, none more so than the Rivonia Trial of 1964.

Introduction

It's clear to me that there's a lot of unfinished business that we all carry in different ways. We will be dealing with the past of this country for the next 100 years, and I suppose that in our Western way, we tend to say, 'We've done that, it's time to move on,' but the past always comes back to bite us.

Fr Michael Lapsley, 2004
In April 1990, in the dying days of apartheid, Fr Lapsley lost
both hands and an eye to a letter bomb sent to him in Zimbabwe.

T he one thing that constantly looms large in South Africa's future is South Africa's past. Hardly a day goes by without something being said, often casually, that reminds people of how it was, how normal, how abnormal. It's always an arguable condition. If South Africans can agree on the essential facts, that's often where the agreement ends. After all, who you were – or were thought to be by the texture of your hair or the colour of your skin – made a world of difference, and, in many ways, still does.

The history of the past century, the fifty years that led up to apartheid, and the fifty years of its rise and fall, remains a zone of discomfort as much in public politics as in private memory and imagination. It is true for all human history that the past is obstinately present, an inescapable shadow of accumulated yesterdays nobody can quite shake off. But perhaps the special difficulty with apartheid lies in the dissonance of remembering.

For many, their stories of apartheid are conceivably inexhaustible, while others will wonder what more can possibly be said. How much longer, they will ask, can we dwell on all that? Aren't the present and the future demanding enough? The exasperation embedded in this contradiction – the untiring accounting against the desire to put an end to it – arises possibly from a sense that there can be no such thing as enough; enough recalling, or atoning, or, indeed, of going back to make better sense of it. Even those who find themselves on the 'wrong' side in conversations about the past, appearing either bravely or hopelessly to be

attempting a defence of sorts, or trying to get at this or that subtle point to show that 'it' wasn't all bad, or 'they' weren't strictly heartless, will feel this deprivation of attention. The same is true for the serious-minded few, conscious of the risks of allowing sentiment to run away with history, who show cool determination in testing orthodoxies that obscure often unexpected truths.

Doubtless, the victims of apartheid continue to feel it all the more urgently, especially as memorable events recede and with them, possibly, the clarity of emotion, or the public acknowledgement of how it felt at the time. For all the millions of words of testimony and recollection, admission, apology, protest and revision, the intimate confessions and the banal records of an extraordinary South African 'ordinariness', the idea of completion, of calling it a day and putting a lid on the constant seep of stories, is somehow impermissible.

But it may be that it is impermissible less because of a need to match some moral requirement of sustaining pity, shame or guilt than for the sobering fact that 'apartheid' itself is not wholly spent. It is not as if anyone is cynically conspiring to breathe new life into it – or could, even if they wished to – but that despite its failure and its constitutional defeat, the accretion of its consequences continues to shape the lives and thoughts, the expectations and the reach even

The idea that Afrikaners and English-speakers stood united to defend the British empire, expressed in this 1914 cartoon from the *Rand Daily Mail*, concealed the deep divisions that persisted after Union in 1910.

of people who were, as they say, 'born free', born after the fact. The motive force itself, the object of fascination and shame – whatever it was, exactly – is not yet exhausted. In many ways, if only because past and future can only ever be a continuum, South Africa is still living an apartheid narrative, and even, in perverse ways, recreating it. It remains the story of our time.

* * *

Formally speaking, as a political programme, apartheid only began in 1948, though the term itself originated some time earlier, in the late 1920s. But the notions that impelled it, chiefly that what made people meaningfully – and usefully – distinctive was the colour of their skin, were a long time in the making.

In the early 2000s, when interest in the quest for the key to human identity was heightened by the sequencing of the human genome, human geneticist Trefor Jenkins of the University of the Witwatersrand offered a telling insight into the history of the differentiation of world populations. While skin colour had been the iconic feature of 'race' for as long as travellers noticed that populations living far away looked different from them, Jenkins observed, early travellers proceeding slowly, mostly by land, did not assign any special meaning to morphological differences in the peoples they encountered. He found that while Herodotus in the 5th century BC, Marco Polo in the 13th century and Ibn Battutah in the 14th, described both skin colour and the appearance of the people they met, they 'categorized them by culture and religion only – as "idolaters" or "infidels", for instance – not in categories grounded in physical appearance.'

There was no general term for race in the modern sense before long-distance ocean travel began in the mid-15th century. With seaborne exploration, the weeks or months of isolation that separated the familiarity of home from the strangeness of far shores yielded vivid observations about the physical appearance of newly encountered fellow humans. It was only in 1758 that Linnaeus classified *Homo sapiens* into four sub-species: *H sapiens europaeus*, *H sapiens afer* (West Africa), *H sapiens asiaticus* (Indonesia) and *H sapiens americanus* (northeast North America). Johann Blumenbach, a German medical doctor and comparative anatomist, distinguished in 1775 between people of south-east and north-east Asia, naming his collection of European skulls 'Caucasoid' because he considered those from the Caucasus mountains to be 'beautiful', the most perfectly formed specimens, implying superiority.

In this way, observed differences were matched to a hierarchy of classification imposed in the service of what later came to be called 'power relations' exercised by agents of change, men (mainly) who possessed ships, guns, horses, knowledge of the latest science, and the written word, and were part of an enterprise in which trade, conquest and exploitation were by and large the assumptions of progress.

Genetic science's thorough disarming of customary notions of racial genetics – the fiction of black genes or white genes, for instance – and its revelation of a common human chemistry that obliterated the concept of supposed racial predispositions to superiority or inferiority, came at the end of a century in which racism had sunk to its atrocious nadir in Nazi anthropology and the genocide it sought to justify.

It's a matter of grim fascination that at the very moment of Nazism's defeat, South Africa embarked on a mammoth social experiment that seemed to owe much to the brutish racial pieties of Nazi theorists. And yet this is almost certainly a deceiving association that obscures, more than explains, how apartheid came to be, and what it actually was.

*　*　*

By the second half of the 1700s, the essentials of modern southern African history – the emergence of a new and evolving regional society formed by contests over land and resources – were well established. The geography, wherever it could sustain life, was peopled variously by a permanent and spreading native white population of European descendants, a substantial community of slaves, the remnants of an all but decimated indigenous population of hunter-gatherers and herders, and legions of black farmers who, over centuries, had penetrated southward from central Africa.

On all their doings was exerted the alien force of faraway colonial administrations, first Dutch, later British, whose political and economic designs – which invariably matched the interests of the white natives – drew soldiers, engineers, missionaries and traders into new and changing relationships with the landscape and the people in it.

The long presence of slaves in the Cape, and – when slavery was abolished in the 1830s – the mass departure for the interior of white farmers in the Great Trek, decisively influenced the social and political values in the region and sharpened the contests over living space and resources.

From the earliest days, access to water and grazing was the nub of competition and, where one or the other side dug in its heels, combat. Through resistance, conquest or flight, the patterns of expanding settlement brought ever-greater areas of the region into a whole, whose interrelated parts were claimed or occupied by inhabitants of contrasting customs, history, language, belief and appearance. What they shared was a dependence on the same basic needs, the limits of their common humanness. And survival often meant taking sides, finding strength in numbers, by identity or alliance.

Clan, tribal or ethnic identities and affinities formed and reformed as claims to agricultural and, later, mineral and economic assets were staked or challenged. To varying degrees, ingenuity, greed, common sense, even altruism, stimulated leaders and followers as they tried to make their way in constantly changing conditions. Violence was ever-present.

There was not a decade without armed conflict in the bloody 100 years of the pacification and then unification of the region, from Britain's second and lasting occupation of 1806 to Union in 1910, which formalised the single multi-province state of South Africa. From a distance, it's tempting to sketch the historical social behaviour of southern Africa to show that under the pressure of conflict, when communities felt compelled to take sides – as people always do when a fight is in the offing – the default option was always racial identity. Often enough, the distinctions between communities – though the blurring of the edges was already considerable, and would grow – could be drawn along the lines of 'race' as defined by skin colour. Broadly speaking, interests coincided, or seem from a distance to have coincided, with epidermal shading.

Yet many of the conflicts, and certainly the greatest and most costly of them, the South African War of 1899-1902, demonstrate the reverse. Not only was that war the most devastating instance of white-on-white violence – to borrow a phrase from the late apartheid years – but it was one in which all communities were embroiled, or played a part, if often unwillingly, in ways not predicated on skin colour or any obvious racial affinity.

However, where the conflict deepened the ethnic division in the white community between Afrikaner and English South Africans it stimulated a brand of nationalism that deepened racial division; the welling of 'Boer War' grievance in the ensuing decades was indispensable to the uniting of Afrikaners around the idea of ethnic supremacy ultimately embodied in apartheid.

The peace extracted in 1902 from the militarily and morally exhausting war – an enterprise tarnished by its origins in Britain's hankering for the gold reefs of Paul Kruger's Witwatersrand, and, especially, by the deaths of thousands of women and children in callously mismanaged concentration camps – presented its inheritors with the challenge of husbanding a new state into being and getting it onto its productive feet as painlessly as possible.

The primary objective of overcoming what was called, ironically, the 'race problem' (the schism between English and Afrikaner communities) so transfixed delegates to the National Convention that met in 1908 and 1909, that, with a nod from Britain, they hammered out a compromise founded on deferring for the time being the greater difficulty of the 'native problem'. And, in the years from Union in 1910 to the turning-point election of 1948, black rights and dignity steadily diminished.

*   *   *

South Africa's 'native problem', no less than its 'race problem', was, arguably, a difficulty of intimacy rather than of strangeness. If the intimacies were seldom actually affectionate, they amounted to a familiarity that registered in the growth of social and economic interdependence.

The wars, treks and treaties of the 1800s, quite as much as the toiling on farm, mine and factory floor, produced a more or less indivisible society in which no section could go it alone. This was more obvious than ever when, in 1947, the Pimville squatter leader Oriel Monongoaha likened Jan Smuts's United Party government to a farmer whose cornfield has been invaded by birds: 'He chases the birds from one part of the field and they alight in another part,' Monongoaha mused. 'We shall see whether it is the farmer or the birds who gets tired first …'

The inevitable tiring he foresaw, the resignation to the reality of a common belonging which no amount of chasing around will alter, echoes the earlier conception of South Africans' indivisible interests penned by the novelist Olive Schreiner in *Thoughts on South Africa* (1923):

> *Wherever a Dutchman, an Englishman, a Jew, and a native are superimposed, there is a common South African condition through which no dividing line can be drawn … South African unity is not the dream of a visionary; it is not even the forecast of genius … South African unity is a condition of practical necessity which is daily and hourly forced upon us by the common needs of life; it is the one path open to us.*

A hard fact of life this common South African condition may have been, yet, she argued, it would require determined political leadership to give it substance and direction:

> *For this unity all great men born in South Africa during the next century will be compelled directly and indirectly to labour; it is this unity which must precede the production of anything great and beautiful by our people as a whole; neither art, nor*

science, nor literature, nor statecraft will flourish among us as long as we remain in our unorganised form: it is the attainment of this unity which constitutes the problem of South Africa: How, from our political states and our discordant races, can a great, a healthy, a united, an organised nation be formed?

It is an ideal – or a truth – that the bulk of South Africans, and certainly all their political organisations (with the exception, perhaps, of the Liberal Party, which disbanded rather than be compelled to fail the test) have struggled to live up to, even those avowedly committed to non-racialism.

When it came to knowing who you were and being certain of your identity, whatever common patriotism may have been felt from time to time – perhaps in heady moments during the two world wars, or on rare occasions when a sporting team garnered more than usually unprejudiced hurrahs – the distinction most people fell back on invariably defined them as a member of this or that language group or 'race'.

As a general rule, South Africans' common condition has always been muddled by other notions of identity, of being more at ease with a narrower, more comfortable – an 'own' – sense of belonging. A telling and quite poignant reflection of this emerges from the childhood recollections of former president FW de Klerk, the undoubtedly courageous Nationalist leader who helped devise and preside over the dismantling of the apartheid state. When the De Klerks lived on a smallholding outside Krugersdorp in the 1940s, as he recalls in his autobiography, *The Last Trek: A New Beginning*, 'my best playmates were the young sons of the black farmhands who worked for my father'. They swam together in the dam, hunted birds and played clay-stick shooting, a pattern of childhood fraternalism not uncommon to many white and black South Africans:

My best friend was Charlie, whose father, Jackson, looked after my father's cattle and whose mother, Anna, did our washing. However, in those days, such friendships ended at the kitchen door. When my parents called me for dinner, Charlie went his way and I went mine. This seemed to me at the time – and probably also to him – to be the natural course of life.

It was, of course, determined by history and habit, and, not many years after 1948, it was intensified by design.

De Klerk remembers that while he and his fellow Afrikaner friends felt 'no animosity' towards black children – 'just a strong sense of difference' – their relations with English-speaking children were jarred by 'strongly anti-British' feeling. This was a sentiment critical to the gestation of apartheid. Ironically, one of apartheid's consequences was a cementing of the interests of English and Afrikaner at the expense of those black playmates left behind in innocent childhoods.

A complementary footnote to De Klerk's childhood recollections is his acknowledgement of an early forebear, Diana of Bengal, who was brought to southern Africa as a slave. This, he notes, was 'a part of my genealogy of which we did not speak – and of which I did not know – when I was a child'. Such racial admixture is a common enough feature of South African family histories – and, according to genealogical research, of all Afrikaner families – but when so much was riding on 'pure' racial identity it was rarely owned up to. What you called yourself, or what others called you, determined virtually everything about how you lived.

Even in the 21st century, South Africans reach with easy familiarity for identities forged for them by historical figures they loathe, values they reject or forces they regard as spent. It is one of the ways in which the ghost of apartheid still haunts boardroom, shebeen, sports team and dinner party, and those long, impressively patient, determined lines of voters on election days. Asking South Africans to change their political allegiance is still often akin to asking them to deny who they are. But it is not universally true, or fixed, today, and it was not universally true of the past either.

* * *

Durable historical assumptions – arguably a measure of the success of apartheid thinking – tend to dilute with scepticism our reading of the account of National Party MP Bruckner de Villiers being carried shoulder-high into Parliament by coloured supporters who, in the 1929 election, had helped him secure the Stellenbosch seat. It's as if, knowing what we do about Afrikaner nationalism, or of the seemingly obvious political options of those perceived to be its victims, such a thing cannot have been true, even in the pre-apartheid late 1920s. Nationalists, more than anyone else, put paid to such apparently unlikely emblems of unprejudiced politics by fastidiously defining belonging by race and, thus, removing the opportunities for their exhibition.

The assertion of Afrikaner ethnicity, of which apartheid was both the means and the end, forged solidarity and new alliances among its subjects or victims, and, in time, among its beneficiaries, even those who claimed to – and actually did – oppose it. Increasingly, South African truths could be spelled out, and made sense of, in black and white.

Historian William Beinart observes that '[e]ven if biological racism was not explicitly part of Nationalist rhetoric, its crude assumptions suffused everyday white language.' Promoters of apartheid traded on fear, of domination or of the imagined consequences of racial mixing. 'The killing blow in a white political argument,' he writes, 'was, put delicately: would you let your daughter marry a black man?'

The meanness of such reductions, and the outraged attention they attracted, meant, often, that the rise of Afrikaner nationalism earned moral rather than historical analysis, or that dispassionate investigation of the data often gave way to altogether more useful – self-serving or self-defining – indignation.

One of the more interesting and penetrating assessments of the origins and nature of Afrikaner nationalism – and one that 'went beyond moral indignation', as Hermann Giliomee and Bernard Mbenga note in their *New History of South Africa* – was Jordan Ngubane's book, *An African Explains Apartheid*, published in 1963:

Apartheid is too complex to be dismissed as a mere political outlook or an ideological aberration. It is seen primarily as a way of life evolved in unusual circumstances for the purpose of guaranteeing survival to the Afrikaner and winning his right to a place in the South African sun. Fundamentalism, absolutism, repudiation, and race hatred are the main pillars of this life – not because the Afrikaner is incorrigibly backward, wicked, dishonest, or callous, but because they are integral parts of the only political heritage it was his lot to inherit from history. The trek into the interior and the decades in the wild plains of southern Africa cut him off from the mainstream of European civilisation. His numerical weakness exposed him to the danger of extinction. And the turbulent events overseas, liberalised European attitudes in the 18th and 19th centuries, bypassed him: he was fighting for survival against Dingane, Moshoeshoe and Sekhukhuni. His guarantee of security in this situation was to hold on to whatever was his own with a fierce tenacity; the fundamentalist dynamic, group exclusiveness, self-consciousness, repudiation, the temper of the slave owner, a blind love for his people, language and history, and fearlessness. These were integral parts of his culture and make-up, and their validity sprang from the fact that they had brought him to his moment of fulfilment …

Only when the Afrikaner nationalist saw that apartheid threatened his survival, Ngubane predicted, would he change his mind. And he was right. Schreiner was right, too. And yet, perhaps for the very reasons Ngubane identified, her truth would be resisted for decades.

But was it really just about Afrikaner nationalism, its special resentments and confined history forging a radical political narrative for which Afrikanerdom

Apartheid planners imagined white South Africa's future wellbeing could be guaranteed by racial segregation, even on buses.

could – or can – be held accountable? Apartheid has always been different things to different people, not least to historians, many of whom felt themselves compelled to choose sides, less as a consequence of scholarship than of conscience. In this way, the contest of ideas about the history of apartheid was, or became – or could not be anything other than – a moral one.

There were those who argued that it was precisely the Afrikaner, with his old-fashioned, slave-owning values, biblical, hidebound ideas and frontier conservatism born of fear of attack and defeat, who brought apartheid into being. Along with this view was that the alternative of modernity, liberal kindliness and confidence in civilised ideas would correct South Africa's history and enable gradual, peaceful change. Others saw it very differently; to them, apartheid was aligned with capitalist interests, and the conflict was not ethnic, or even strictly racial, but a class contest in which all whites – even, or especially, the liberal ones and the benign West to which they paid allegiance – benefited by exerting political, and thus economic, dominance over the majority. To them, profits rather than principles determined the evolution of white-dominated, class-based politics. In the later period of apartheid, these positions often defined the binary argument about who was to blame, and who deserved to win, and how.

This 'liberal' versus 'radical' controversy was closely studied by American scholar Harrison M Wright, who observed in *The Burden of the Present*, first published in 1977, that 'wherever urgent contemporary social issues … weigh too heavily on the thin and complex web of hypothesis, evidence, analysis and imaginative recreation with which historians construct their understanding of the past … history becomes less a study of the past than a weapon of the present'. It was a 'major failing' of all schools of history in South Africa that there was often an 'unwillingness, in the pursuit of causes, to recognise the extraordinary complexity of the South African past'. The challenge facing historians, he argued, was to

try to understand the web of circumstances in which past people found themselves … [and] that impersonal and uncontrollable social forces often determine the course of a society's development, that reasoned social action does not always have the results intended and that there are not always particular individuals or particular groups that can be held responsible for every social problem or for every example of human misery.

It is a weakness that has been offset before and since by independent-minded historians, who have mined the depths of familiar episodes to bring to the surface sometimes unexpected data and insights. More than thirty years after Wright's book was first published, historian Bill Nasson examined the apartheid experience in his 2010 inaugural lecture at the University of Stellenbosch, with a view to testing the tenacious idea of South Africa's 20th-century abnormality, and the certainties about its history. Along with 'familiar apartheid truths', he noted, were other historical truths that remained true 'even if they are unfamiliar'. South Africa was not, for instance, 'completely without … the usual rhythms of modern history'. An examination of demography or population history showed, predictably enough, that apartheid had had 'devastating long-term consequences', yet also revealed altogether less likely 'progressive historical transitions': 'From about three million people in 1880, South Africa had some 44 million in 2000. This period was one of almost continuously rising life expectancy, except for a slight dip in the 1918 influenza epidemic and, obviously, during the most recent years of AIDS attrition.' But, compared to the war mortality and ethnic bloodbaths in Europe's 20th century, 'the abnormal thing about this country, speaking demographically, has been the security of human life … Even in the most mercilessly repressive stage of the anti-apartheid insurgency, life remained more secure than it had been in much of … twentieth-century Europe'. Over a little more than a century, Nasson observed, 'mortality has declined, fertility has dropped, and households have become smaller. Urbanisation has increased, the proportion of agricultural work in total employment has declined, and the average level of education of the adult population has been rising. In any contemporary historical perspective, this is the standard portrayal of trends in all industrial societies …' It was 'only in its apartheid turn that South Africa became the true continental abnormality. In that, what matters is not merely the exceptional length and depth of its centuries of colonisation [but] that it went on abnormally, for longer than anywhere else.'

* * *

In the early years of apartheid, Nationalist leaders were obsessed about ensuring that their project would, in a phrase, last longer than anywhere else. Often, their own forecasts revealed their uncertainties and delusions about its intended eternity. In a town hall meeting in Beaufort West in August 1952, Eric Louw, then Minister of Economic Affairs, asked: 'What is going to be the position of the small white minority in the year 2052, when the landing of Jan van Riebeeck should again be celebrated? Will the white man still be in the position he is in today?' Needless to say, his gist was that in apartheid alone lay the guarantee that 'the position of the white man can be maintained, politically as well as socially'.

The future is always the torment of nationalists, for the world doesn't stand still, and the natural flux of society seems destined to erode their certainties. In the defiant idealism of their present, nationalists (no less, of course, than their social-engineering soul mates on the left) crave the assurance of succeeding tomorrows whose anticipated validation of the work in progress calls for near-fanatical endurance and an unswerving commitment to the fixed scheme.

The setback, the disappointment, the hold-up, are not taken as warnings from history, but merely as proof of the need to redouble every effort. Thus, in 1950, Hendrik Verwoerd was able to remark: 'Always we have said that the road of apartheid is a long road … People assert that if, at the end of the next fifty years, six million natives will still be in the white areas, that proves we have jettisoned our policy of apartheid. It is untrue … The year 2000 is one of the stations on the road to our ideal. It is not the end …' Yet, despite this outwardly confident assertion, for Afrikaner nationalists in the mid-20th century, the torment of their future was a torment of sums, the definition of their ethnic nationalism – the guarantee, as they saw it, of their survival as a *volk* – condemning them to the status of a numerical minority in a social, political and economic setting dominated by an overwhelming black majority.

Back in 1938, when Afrikaners were re-enacting the Great Trek and contemplating the sorry state of their 'nation' as the economically inferior inheritors of the fruits of Union, it was their own distinctness within the white community, and their own strength in numbers in this limited but important context, that mattered. The Trek centenary, as journalist Schalk Pienaar described it, 'made the volk mightily aware of its very existence'. But it was an awareness of acute vulnerability too.

Afrikaans had been acknowledged as an official language in 1925, and a new flag gave as much attention to the standards of the old Boer republics as to the Union Jack, but, economically, Afrikaners were at the bottom of the pile.

By 1936, half of South Africa's one million Afrikaners were urbanised, but not many first-generation, city-dwelling Afrikaners had the skills or experience for urban jobs. Few Afrikaners made it through their schooling; a tiny number went to university. Signal economic successes had been achieved through companies such as Nasionale Pers, Santam and Sanlam (launched before 1920), Iscor and Escom (in the 1920s) and Volkskas (1934). But, by the late 1930s, the representation of Afrikaner companies in the economy remained slim – one percent in mining, three percent in manufacturing, eight percent in trade and commerce and five percent in the financial sector. There were just 20 Afrikaner business enterprises in all of Johannesburg, and by 1939 only three percent of Afrikaners held jobs in the professions.

Inevitably, given the economic conditions under which they battled to find their way in a modernising, fast-urbanising society – competing with the black poor of the cities for the only jobs they were qualified for – their grievances and vulnerability became closely aligned with an often fierce racial consciousness, and the sense that in their whiteness lay an unquestionable advantage. This was fertile ground for nationalistic activism, especially in the 1930s and 1940s, and the basis of steadily growing support for National Party policy after 1948. Ethnic supremacy was the key driver, but, as William Beinart observes, the 'rhetoric of cultural solidarity sat easily with racial exclusivity and the use of ethnic power for economic gain.'

* * *

The story of the genesis of apartheid is also, in an important sense, the story of the failure of resistance to it.

From before Union in 1910 – and, more intensely, after – racial discrimination and the structuring of the economy to benefit whites, broadly speaking, at the expense of blacks, was challenged by a range of organisations representing people who were not white. Some of them tried to check, or alter by persuasion, the Union constitution that was the key to 20th-century white supremacy. These efforts were brushed aside. In response, two years later, the South African Native National Congress (later the African National Congress) was formed to better organise resistance to growing inequality. Unions played an important role – as they would, again, in later decades – in exerting a resistant force on behalf of black people.

But one law after the next, from the 1913 Natives Land Act and the Mines and Works Amendment Act (the 'colour bar' law) of 1924 to the notorious laws of 1936 (deepening land dispossession, tightening influx control and removing black voters from the voters' roll), steadily narrowed the scope for the argument that equality was desirable and achievable.

In 1935, in a fresh effort to forge a united front, more than 400 delegates from a range of black organisations banded together to form the All African

South African Native National Congress delegates – from left, Thomas Mapike, Rev Walter Rubusana, Rev John Dube, Saul Msane and Sol Plaatje – on the eve of a visit to England in 1914 to seek support for their cause.

Convention, but it was all too gentlemanly, too accommodating. As historian Nigel Worden notes, its 'tactics of petition and moderate reformism differed little from earlier methods and it met with as little response from the government as the South African Native National Congress in 1912'.

Black resistance would not amount to much until the war years, when strike-minded unions and squatter movements began to demonstrate a consciousness among black people of their power to weigh on the white world. White politics mattered in the first half of the 20th century because, by design, it was the dominant socio-political narrative against which there was no countervailing force to speak of. Ironically, almost, it was precisely an acceptance of the hard facts of the South African reality – the preponderance, if not yet the dominance, of black people by sheer force of numbers – that lent urgency and direction to the development of apartheid.

In the torment of sums was also the solution, or the perceived solution – the compelling argument that so long as Afrikaners banded together around the core principle of ethnic preservation, they would survive. And the persuasive idea of 'apartheid' – suitably vague and elastic as a policy, but catchy as a concept – did the trick. Radicals and moderates, emergent industrialists and blue-collar workers, intellectuals, clerics, tenant farmers and estate owners rallied to the cause of former dominee DF Malan's National Party (NP) to defeat Jan Smuts's moderate United Party (UP) government in 1948.

On the face of it, while justly credited for his part in helping the Allies defeat European fascism, and being eager to see South Africa play its part in standing up to international oppression, Smuts had, out of a kind of domestic complacency, been defeated in turn by similarly reactionary tendencies at home. But it was much more complex than that. For a start, it was only among a minority of Afrikaners that truly cousinly pro-Nazi sentiments ever took root. And, if the election was a rude shock for the UP, the signs of things to come had been obvious for some time.

Some said Smuts brought the disaster on himself by not listening to advisers who had urged him to postpone the election until October when a fresh round of constituency demarcations would favour the UP. The overconfident ruling party was also notoriously complacent about the risks of a united Afrikaner nationalism, convincing itself that its fractious opposition would never get its act together. Yet, while it's true that Afrikanerdom was never as monolithic or single-minded as it was often portrayed as being, it is doubtful whether at any time after the end of the Second World War the gathering force of Afrikaner nationalism could have been evaded or deflected by election strategy, timing or rational persuasion.

Shocking though the outcome of the election was – its impact being compared to a 'bombshell' or 'earth tremor' – the political forces that produced it had been developing over a much longer period. Their origins can be traced to the constructing of an Afrikaner identity from the second half the 1800s and the steady if gradual definition of anti-British grievance from the Jameson Raid of 1895, of which the South African War was a costly consequence. This simmering anger was deftly rekindled by nationalist leaders during the 1938 re-enactment of the Great Trek, marking the centenary of the defining instance of anti-British resistance and the creation of a mythology of righteous Afrikaner republicanism in southern Africa.

In the decade and a half preceding the National Party's coming to power, two convulsive international episodes, the post-1929 Depression and the Second World War, decisively shaped the politics of the Union. The first deepened Afrikaner poverty, the second, Afrikaner grievance. When the Depression reached across the Atlantic, it was felt with a particularly sharp impact by unskilled and ill-educated poor rural Afrikaners who, when they streamed to the cities in the hope of finding work and the chance of a better life, found they were competing directly with poor black people in similar straits. And when, in September 1939, South Africa entered the war against Germany, to the Afrikaners' poverty was added the humiliation of being, once more, under Britain's yoke. Nationalists stewed with resentment when, after the narrow parliamentary majority of just 13 votes sealed South Africa's participation in what they regarded as a British war in Europe, their request for an election to put the question to the country was denied.

Radical organisations that sprang up – such as the pro-Nazi Ossewabrandwag and the New Order – were dead set on fomenting insurrection, and were encouraged by the Allies' early setbacks in the war. Thousands of Afrikaners volunteered to fight in Smuts's army, but even among moderates the manner in which South Africa was harnessed to British interests rubbed old hurts.

And, on the home front, race consciousness was heightened when, with the collapse of wartime imports and the stimulation of local manufacturing, the ever-growing black population of the cities benefited from new economic opportunities created by the departure to the battlefields of thousands of whites, and some expedient relaxation of racial obstacles to work in urban areas.

In the Afrikaner nationalist mind, the departures from accustomed segregation signalled the influence of the long-settled, wealthier, better qualified English-speaking community in whom most Afrikaners felt they dared not place their trust; the English section, many of them felt, could afford to make liberal concessions to black people – whether out of political conviction or economic expedience – because their wealth and standing insured them against the effects. Thus, nurturing racial consciousness was, in one view, part of the Nationalists' strategy to see through its republican ambition of throwing off the yoke of British domination, of finally winning the 'Boer War'.

In the second half of the 1940s, with the war won and anti-British sentiment having lost some traction – even republican-minded Afrikaners joined the cheering crowds during the Royal Visit of 1947 – the Nationalists consolidated their focus on Afrikaner perceptions of racial vulnerability, their sense that 'white survival' was threatened. It wasn't a new theme by any means.

A decade earlier, DF Malan created a powerful image of Afrikaner racial solidarity when he said: 'South Africa expects of its poor whites that they remain white and live white.' A contemporary study contained this striking portrait of the poor Afrikaner of the 1930s and 1940s:

> His poverty, servitude and desperate search for work feeds a sense of dependency and inferiority … Feeling himself unwelcome, he presents himself poorly, he is timid, walks hat in hand and lacks … self-confidence … He wields no influence and no one intercedes on his behalf; his people is small and subordinate … He is despised and treated as an inferior …

This could, in most respects, have been a description of the plight of many poor blacks. That the grievances and hardships of Afrikaners and of black people were comparable, if not exactly alike, was, far from providing common ground for mutual understanding, possibly the very reason for heightened contest. Their white skins, rather than their skills, were the poor whites' only protection, and a handy purchase for Malan's ambition of consolidating nationalist unity around the far-reaching idea that his people must 'live white'.

The scene was set for a major test. It came down to a choice – for white South Africans – between two views of the future spelled out in studies commissioned just before the 1948 election. On Smuts's side, the report by Judge Henry Fagan concluded that racial segregation was impractical and black urbanisation was a fact of life, and that the best thing would be to accept that blacks and whites were 'economically intertwined … and part of the same big machine'. Fagan's report shied away from proposing a master plan, recommending instead 'constant adaptation to changing conditions' and the 'smoothing out of difficulties … so that all may make their contribution and combine their energies for the progress of South Africa'.

On Malan's side, the internal party report by Paul Sauer – which historian Hermann Giliomee has described as being 'characterised by apartheid's peculiar combination of racism and rectitude' – rejected racial equality, proposed wide-ranging segregation between whites and coloureds, and put forward the ultimate ideal of complete apartheid between whites and blacks. This was tempered by an acknowledgement that, for years to come, the white economy would depend on black labour. But the Sauer vision of a systematically divided country was the vision behind the post-1948 Nationalist programme.

The ruling United Party's failure to manage the consequences of urbanisation chiefly for blacks and for Afrikaners – or to develop a clear policy alternative to reinforce the desirability of the inevitable social and economic integration of all South Africans – rendered it incapable of providing convincing leadership for a white electorate that was more conscious than ever of its numerical inferiority in racial terms, and which, in the election campaign of 1948, was presented by the National Party with an unembarrassed 'solution' in the form of apartheid.

At the same time, the constraints of white politics, which it felt compelled to heed, reduced the UP's scope for engaging meaningfully with increasingly demanding, better organised and more militant black politicians. With mounting disenchantment, black people witnessed most of white South Africa's unwillingness to emulate at home its much-honoured contribution to the fight for freedom against oppression in Europe. Where the Nationalists were declarative, confident and convincing – to most Afrikaners, anyway – Smuts and the UP seemed uncertain, indecisive and ill-prepared. If the Nationalists had the simpler task of rallying race- or *volk*-conscious whites, and did so in the election campaign with such brutish slogans as '*Die kaffer op sy plek*' (keep kaffirs in their place) and '*Die koelies uit die land*' (expel the Indians), the UP had to try to balance a wider spectrum of white opinion with the compelling interests of a black majority that was showing signs of appreciating just how powerful it actually was, and which had, under wartime conditions, become indispensably embedded in the economy.

Paralysis threatened the ruling party. It seemed to know what it should do, but did not feel it had any room to manoeuvre. Smuts's right-hand man, the liberal Jan Hofmeyr, wrote to his leader in 1946 after the usually compliant Natives' Representative Council unexpectedly demanded the repeal of discriminatory laws: 'It means that the moderate intellectuals are now committed to an extreme line against colour discrimination and have carried the chiefs with them. We can't afford to allow them to be swept into the extremist camp, but I don't see what we can do to satisfy them, which would be tolerated by European public opinion.'

Even in opposition, some four months after losing to the NP, Smuts himself revealed the disabling indistinctness of the UP when, sparring with his nemesis Malan in a debate, he said: 'We have always stood and we stand for social and residential separation in this country, and for the avoidance of all racial mixture.' When Malan interjected, 'Is that your apartheid?' Smuts responded with the telling concession that 'there is a great deal about apartheid that is common to all parties', offering as the apparently sole defining feature of the UP opposition that 'we see no reason to change the political rights, small as they are, of the Native people and the Coloured people of this country. The small position they have in the parliament of this country, let them keep … let them have their say here too.'

It didn't sound very impressive at all.

Smuts's politics was Fabian, or gradualist. And his main interest lay in holding the middle ground of moderate Afrikaner/English unity, which had been the chief objective of Union in 1910, replacing the bloody hostility of the South African War with carefully nurtured amity based on their shared interests as white-skinned South Africans. After 1948, the highest cost of putting off the difficult decisions on black political rights – steadily eroded from 1910 to the 1930s – was paid by black people themselves. The immediate cost was paid by Smuts; the pace of events had rendered gradualism ineffectual – unappealing to whites, and unappeasing to blacks. Middle-of-the-road South Africanism was swept away by the force of Afrikaner nationalism united as never before by an almost fantastic idea – the reversal of history. The apartheid era had begun.

CHAPTER ONE

Division
by decree

1948-55

Crowds gather in Freedom Square, Fordsburg, on 6 April 1952 to hear ANC leader James Moroka and Yusuf Dadoo of the Indian Congress call for volunteers in the Defiance Campaign against apartheid legislation.

L ate on the afternoon of 27 May 1948, the small group of party officials – though only one of the candidates – who had assembled in the magistrate's court at Standerton, greeted the news of the constituency result in complete silence. 'You could have cut the atmosphere with a knife,' the unlikely winner recalled later. Wentzel 'Wennie' du Plessis was a political nobody who had not for a moment contemplated actually winning. After all, the standing MP he ousted by just 224 votes was no ordinary opponent, but the Prime Minister himself, Field Marshal Jan Smuts, the great Union conciliator, soldier-statesman and philosopher, a friend to Britain's King George VI and a confidant of Winston Churchill.

But in May 1948, Wentzel du Plessis was one among many candidates who claimed seats across the country on a tide of Afrikaner nationalism that took even the National Party by surprise.

Smuts had seemed all but immovable, the kindly 'Oubaas' of a sensible, united South Africanism, whose international status as a leader during the Second World War and, immediately afterwards, as a mover and shaker in the establishment of the United Nations was matched at home by a soldierly loyalty to his solid if ultimately unimaginative wartime leadership.

Years later, Nelson Mandela reflected that the Nationalist victory 'was a shock' which left him 'stunned and dismayed'. The United Party and Smuts, he wrote, 'had beaten the Nazis, and surely they would defeat the National Party'. On the very day of that turning-point election, he and political colleague Oliver Tambo, who would later share a similar status as an icon of the African nationalist resistance, were at a meeting in Johannesburg where 'we barely discussed the question of a Nationalist government because we did not expect one'.

Nor, indeed, did the Afrikaner nationalists who had rallied behind former dominee and newspaper editor DF Malan to deliver the slim but decisive electoral triumph. The result was a body blow to the prospects of gradual political change favoured by Smuts and the UP, and to the hopes of the black majority that post-war South Africa would follow the pattern of a changing world scene

1948

ANC Youth League sets out its Basic Policy, emphasising the new post-war assertiveness of black protest politics.

28 May DF Malan's National Party wins the general election; apartheid is launched.

September Sam Kahn becomes the first Communist to be elected to Parliament, as the Native Representative of the Western Constituency of the Cape, beating a Nationalist and an independent opponent.

1949

Citizenship Act extends to five years the period after which British subjects may become South Africans.

Prohibition of Mixed Marriages Act bars marriages between 'whites and non-whites'.

in which equality and freedom from oppression were dominant themes. From this election, the country turned its back on all that, and began the complex, costly experiment of making its own history. If its authors were a minority – even, in fact, a minority of the white population – the environment that gave them their wholly unexpected opportunity in the first election after the war was a larger sum of national and international forces, a long history of race consciousness and discrimination and the competing pressures of black and Afrikaner grievance.

It is a telling footnote of the Standerton contest, which ended Smuts's career as a statesman, that Wentzel du Plessis, a former diplomat, had been dismissed some years earlier because he had refused to resign his membership of the Afrikaner Broederbond, as Smuts had ordered in an instruction to Union civil servants. Whether Du Plessis's challenge of 1948 was an avenging one or not, it was when the electrifying bulletin – 'Smuts beaten at Standerton' – was hammered out on the clattering telex machines in newspaper offices across the country that the full impact of Nationalist gains hit home.

Smuts was spared the humiliation of his opponents' cheers outside the Standerton court; even before polls had closed the day before he had returned to his home at Irene, near Pretoria, where, 24 hours later, he took the call that confirmed the worst. It is said he betrayed nothing of his inner turmoil, merely saying 'Thank you,' putting the phone down and returning to his chair. But there was consternation among officials, who delayed the public announcement of the result until late in the evening, evidently in deference to the old man's feelings – even though the news had spread like wildfire, and a telegram had been sent almost immediately to the King to tell him Smuts had lost.

By then, however, Smuts would almost certainly have known that a significant change had come over South Africa, and that he had misjudged the mood of his own people and the potency of their unresolved quest for sovereignty, which he

Once enemies in the South African War, Jan Smuts and Winston Churchill were firm allies in the fight against Nazism.

South West Africa Affairs Amendment Act extends parliamentary representation to whites in the mandated territory.
Native Laws Amendment Act creates labour bureaus intended to restrict flow of black workers to towns.

December ANC adopts Programme of Action, abandoning the moderate approach of petitions and deputations in favour of mass action such as boycotts, strikes and civil disobedience. Walter Sisulu is elected secretary-general and Dr James

Moroka replaces Dr Alfred Xuma as president-general.
December Voortrekker Monument inaugurated.

Grinding poverty and official hostility was the fate of squatter camp residents in the 'white' towns and cities of the 1950s.

had helped fight for as a guerrilla commander in the South African War half a century earlier.

After polls closed on the evening of 26 May, and counting began, the early returns belied the looming upset. By dawn on 27 May, the outlook was unexceptional, with the UP leading with 36 seats to four each for the HNP (the National Party's full name, then, was Herenigde – reunified – Nasionale Party) and the Labour Party. But as the day wore on, and the astonishing percentage poll of 91.2% meant counters had their work cut out for them, the picture began to change.

The first sign of things to come was the loss to the Nationalists of the once safe seat of Losberg. Then, later on, Cabinet minister Piet van der Bijl lost Bredasdorp.

1950
Nelson Mandela succeeds Peter Mda as president of ANC Youth League.

January Communist Party of South Africa holds its last conference before its dissolution.

March Alfred Xuma resigns from the ANC national executive committee over differences with the Youth League.

And so it continued. Of course, many Nats lost; two men who failed to win a seat in 1948 would later loom large in apartheid iconography, each becoming leader of the party, and prime minister. One was Hendrik Verwoerd, the former academic and, latterly, influential editor of *Die Transvaler* newspaper. (He did go to Parliament in 1948, but as a Senate appointee.) The other was John Balthazar Vorster, an Ossewabrandwag internee during the war, who lost Brakpan by just two votes in a contest the UP incumbent had been expected to win with a comfortable majority of 2 000.

In the end, most seats went to the NP. Yet, overall, they won the election on a minority vote, just 37.7% of the turnout at the polls. This garnered 401 834 votes in all, and 70 seats. What made all the difference to Malan was his coalition with Nikolaas Havenga's Afrikaner Party, whose 41 885 votes (3.9%) delivered nine seats more. The United Party was far and away the winner on votes – 524 230, or 49.1% of the electorate – but gleaned only 65 seats. With its allies, the Labour Party (27 360 votes, or 2.5% of the electorate, delivering six seats) and the three Native Representatives, the UP came out five seats short of the Nationalists.

The NP's own more realistic ambitions for power had focused on the 1953 election, five years hence, and even then – though it consolidated its gains – it still didn't earn a majority of white votes. What gave the Nationalists the edge was a constitutional arrangement on constituency demarcation, which allowed rural seats to have fewer voters than urban ones. And the countryside was dominated by Afrikaners. Time and again, in 1948, the NP scraped home, taking seats off the UP by sometimes tiny margins, while the UP piled up extravagant tallies in safe seats. Typical of this pattern was the final result declared at 7.30am on 28 May – a 24-vote Nationalist majority that snatched Victoria West from the UP. The ruling party's fate was sealed.

At his home, Morewag, in Stellenbosch, the outwardly humourless though dogged and astute Daniel Malan assumed the mantle of national leadership with a ringing declaration: 'Today South Africa belongs to us once more. For the first time since Union [1910] South Africa is our own. May God grant that it will always remain our own.'

From an Afrikaner nationalist perspective, Malan rescued the cause from the diluting effects of JBM Hertzog's coalition with Smuts in the Fusion government

---

1 May General strike against all discriminatory laws and for full franchise. Eighteen people are killed and 30 wounded when police fire on protests in Alexandra and other areas on the Witwatersrand.

20 June Communist Party of South Africa decides it will dissolve itself a few days before the enactment of the Suppression of Communism Act.

26 June Suppression of Communism Act makes the Communist Party illegal.

of the mid-1930s and from the divisive skirmishes with the militant would-be standard-bearers of Afrikaner resistance during the Second World War. Malan's altogether more strategic approach in stimulating Afrikaners' sense of themselves as an embattled racial minority, coupled with his less radical politics – favouring the ballot box rather than insurrection – paid off handsomely in May.

To many Afrikaners, the last battle of the 'Boer War' had been won. To black South Africans, the last, long battle for citizenship, dignity and freedom was about to begin.

*   *   *

The country waited expectantly, and, soon enough, things began to change. An innocent-seeming headline in the *Cape Argus* of August 1948, 'Segregation in Suburban Trains', heralded a new and apparently slightly puzzling alteration to commuting in Cape Town. The report described measures introduced by the Minister of Transport (Paul Sauer, as it happens, author of the NP's apartheid vision), which, in their way, made history; this was the first practical application of apartheid policy.

It was all very disturbing to George Golding, president of the Coloured People's National Union. While it was true the Nationalists had fought the election on this issue, he was quoted as saying, 'the idea of segregation, in the face of the Cape's Liberal colour policy, comes as a great shock to us as a people'. Many still found it hard to believe that the Nationalists really meant to turn back the tide. But Sauer's measures were due within the week.

Cape readers learned there would by no means be 'complete apartheid', but the new regulations would 'consist merely of reserving certain first-class accommodation for Europeans only, and the coaches concerned will carry boards to that effect. So far as is known at present, there will, for a start, be no apartheid in the second-class. The scheme is experimental and may be developed later.' Deceivingly, though rationally enough, the report went on: 'To carry out apartheid fully would mean running double trains, which the railway with their limited rolling stock, track, and staff, are not able to do. In the absence of details it is presumed that the provisions proposed by Mr. Sauer will be as far as the railways can at present go.'

A Day of National Protest and Mourning is held countrywide. 26 June is declared Freedom Day.
July Population Registration Act and Group Areas Act.

December UN General Assembly finds that apartheid 'is necessarily based on doctrines of racial discrimination'.

1951

March DF Malan announces the Separate Representation of Voters Bill to remove coloureds from the common voters' roll in the Cape.

DF Malan poses unsmilingly with his wife, Mana, at their official Pretoria residence, Libertas, in 1953. Paul Sauer (above) was author of the National Party's vague but – to most Afrikaner nationalists – persuasive apartheid vision.

What is evident, and it was true for every other aspect of the new reality, was that nobody really knew what 'apartheid' would actually amount to, how the patent impracticalities would be overcome and how, ultimately, it could ever really mean what it seemed to mean. This lack of definition was part of its strength as an election strategy; it was vague enough to attract support from across all of Afrikaner society, from university professors and ministers of the church to businessmen and wealthy farmers, from the poor folk of the countryside to the artisans, miners and factory workers of the city. It meant complete and systematic racial separation to those who believed that was the least they needed to feel secure and know they had a future. Equally, apartheid also meant a pragmatic acceptance of at least some racial interdependence to those who recognised that white economic wellbeing depended on black labour remaining in towns and cities, not in far-off reserves.

May War Veterans Torch Commando, consisting largely of white ex-servicemen, is formed to oppose Separate Representation of Voters Bill.

June Death of Pixley ka Isaka Seme, a founder member and treasurer-general of the ANC in 1912.

June ANC's national executive committee meets to discuss a joint campaign of civil disobedience and general strikes.

While, on paper, one of the key intended principles was, as Minister of the Interior Dr TE Dönges defined it in a 1948 speech, 'racial separation with equal facilities', the result was, in effect, white supremacy – white interests above all others. To start with, there was a bit of a muddle in NP ranks over quite how to re-engineer state and society, but, conscious of its tenuous hold on power and the need to act decisively to entrench its policies and consolidate its position, the party intended to move as fast as it could, and did.

If, in Smuts's phrasing, 'social and residential separation' and 'the avoidance of all racial mixture' was, broadly, a fair description of how things stood when the Nationalists came to power, existing racial measures were expanded and intensified through rules, regulations, prohibitions, injunctions and proposals that would touch every aspect of life. Segregation on suburban trains was the least of it. New laws and amendments in the parliamentary sessions of 1948 and 1949 set the pattern which had three essential objectives: deepening racial separation; strengthening NP power; and narrowing the scope for protest.

A slow but meaningful start was made in 1948 with amendments withdrawing Indian representation in Parliament and making it more difficult for coloured voters to register – there were some 46 000 on the Cape voters' roll. The beginnings of pro-Afrikaner affirmative action, or preferment, in civil service ranks was signalled by the sudden departure, a month after the election, of the Chief of Staff of the Union Defence Force, Major-General Evered Poole.

In the 1949 sittings, MPs approved a new Citizenship Act to extend from two to five years the period of residence of British subjects before they could become citizens (or voters in the next election); a prohibition on all marriages across colour lines; the creation of labour bureaus to control the flow of black workers to towns; and a new law, defying the terms of the United Nations, giving whites in mandated South West Africa the right to elect MPs to the South African Parliament. The Nationalists were confident most South West African whites would support apartheid too.

* * *

But it was in the third year of NP rule that the all-embracing scale of the enterprise became clear. As Prime Minister DF Malan was telling enthralled patriots at the inauguration of the Voortrekker Monument near Pretoria in December 1949 that it was their duty as the descendants of the heroic trekkers to sustain 'White Christian civilisation' through 'paramountcy' and 'race purity' while acting as 'guardians over the non-European races', his officials and law advisers were putting the finishing touches to the keystone law of the apartheid edifice, the Population Registration Act. This 1950 law classified everybody into three broad categories; 'Europeans' (whites), coloureds and blacks, with coloureds and blacks being more closely classified according to tribal or ethnic associations (Indian, Asian, Zulu, Griqua, Xhosa, Cape Malay, and so on). It provided for identity papers to stamp every person with a declared, and often arbitrary, racial identity. Provision was made for appeals to change a racial classification, and no fewer than 100 000 people rushed to lodge appeals when the law was passed, many thousands of them to save jobs, or marriages. As a doubtful or borderline case, it could be enough to be compelled to undergo the infamous pencil test – the pencil signifying frizzy hair if it stuck when pushed into the subject's hair by a fastidiously indifferent official – to be classified as 'non-European'. And to be classified as non-European was almost always an inescapable penalty.

In a society in which racial or ethnic identities were never so crisp or neat – and had never had to be to this extent – the Population Registration Act severed families, marriages and bonds of love and kinship as husbands and wives, uncles and cousins, friends and neighbours were classified into different racial categories which, from here on, determined everything in life and even death, from maternity home to cemetery. This law became the master template.

The second key law of 1950, the Group Areas Act, applied the crude template of race to the landscape, determining the ownership and occupation of land by skin colour. The main purpose was to make the established precincts of towns and cities white – where in many cases black and coloured people had lived for centuries – and create mean, barren satellite or dormitory townships round the edges, without amenities, jobs or decent transport. In time, hundreds of thousands of people would be the poorly compensated, or never compensated, losers to this measure. The Act fragmented cities and lives and dislocated whole communities from their historical places and the jobs and social values that went with them.

Father Trevor Huddleston writes to Christian Action asking for financial support in defending and assisting the families of Defiance Campaign volunteers.

21 **January** James Moroka and Walter Sisulu write to Malan, who responds through his private secretary, lambasting the ANC for writing to him directly instead of going through the Minister of Native Affairs. The ANC rejects the repudiation.

If Christian righteousness was ever the inspiration of Nationalist piety, it was surely suspended in 1950 when the NP elaborated the 1927 Immorality Act (forbidding sex between whites and blacks) to include sex between whites and any 'non-whites'. Securing convictions – and jail terms – for this new crime gave police licence to snoop, flashing torches into cars and acting on informers' tips even to burst into bedrooms. It led to suicides, heartbreak and thousands of arrests. By the May 1951 court appearance, for instance, of Eldred Bryan Ormonde and Dorothy Jubelin on charges under the Immorality Act (both were found guilty), racial appearance had been not only thoroughly criminalised but made the object of such courtroom hocus-pocus as magistrate DR Jacobs's confident assertion that 'I feel justified in holding that a large percentage of Coloureds have telltale features. They inherit certain physical characteristics like high cheekbones, wide nostrils and black curly hair. If they possess these they can be considered as Coloured within the contemplation of the Act notwithstanding any preponderance of blood.' Thus, it was possible for Jacobs to find of Dorothy Jubelin that her features 'imparted a decidedly Coloured appearance and her light complexion could not sufficiently relieve her from her hereditary disability so as to lull a reasonable European into not suspecting a dusky admixture.'

Ormonde and Jubelin, like so many others, are names that appear briefly and then seem to disappear for good, trampled to nothing in the march of a grand narrative in which human identities, feelings and pleas were made secondary to an increasingly fanatical idea. Since the common law, drawn from ancient Roman, Dutch and English law, was colour-blind, every feature of racial discrimination had to be spelled out in new legislation, corrupting the notion of justice and of normalcy itself.

Soon enough, for all their outrage, liberal newspapers would bring news of the bobbysoxer fad, Elizabeth Taylor's first – of eight – marriages and the latest immorality cases from the magistrates' courts with the equally unalarmed quality of reports from a given world. Even the Anglican Church in Southern Africa found itself in the early 1950s defending segregation at its own schools; Archbishop Geoffrey Clayton argued that 'in a country where there is as much colour prejudice as there is in South Africa, it is probable that a non-European boy or girl would not be happy in a European school ... [and] it would be impossible ...

---

6 April Tercentenary celebrations of Jan van Riebeeck's arrival at the Cape; ANC-led Joint Planning Council holds mass meetings and demonstrations throughout the country in preparation for the Defiance Campaign.

25 May Minister of Justice CR Swart terminates Sam Kahn and Fred Carneson's membership of Parliament and the Provincial Council, respectively, for being Communists.

31 May ANC executive meeting in Port Elizabeth sets the Defiance Campaign's launch date as 26 June.

to ensure that he would be accepted by the other children'.

Obsessive racialism began to generate its own peculiar kinds of – ultimately self-serving – reasoning. 'It is sometimes possible to see dark blood in a person classed as white,' writer Sarah Gertrude Millin observed notoriously in *The People of South Africa* (1951), 'by the dark neck and forehead, the tinged eyeballs – some say, the very thin legs.'

Parliamentary debate was punctuated with outlandish claims and bizarre qualms. In the sitting of 12 May 1950, for instance, Senator DH van Zyl raised the evidently worrisome question of control over the blood transfusion service. If black blood was transfused into the body of a white person, he wondered anxiously, 'what will the biological reaction be?'

Apartheid's hazy notions of reordering society by race were widely satirised – as in this 1953 cartoon, by Umboneli (Gerry Norton) – yet Nationalists demonstrated a near-fanatical conviction in making the fantastic real.

Race law spawned language and logic that defied reason and weakened common decency, inuring growing numbers of white people to the abnormality of their socio-economic reality. This was not a novelty in 1948 or in the preceding years. As Arthur Keppel-Jones pointed out in the introduction to his novelistic cautionary tale, *When Smuts Goes* (1947), South African politics and thought had long been prone to 'deep-rooted tendencies'. At the midpoint of the century, however, these tendencies 'happen at present to find their most unequivocal expression' in the National Party.

Where the brace of laws passed in the first half of the 1950s dispelled any doubt about the Nationalists' programme of rigidly ordering society and economy by race, their determined struggle to remove coloured voters from the common roll betrayed their obsession with power at the lasting cost of democratic traditions and pretensions. Coloured votes, most of which went to Smuts and the United Party in the 1948 election, were significant in at least half of the Cape's 55 seats and possibly decisive in as many as seven. The Nationalists were determined to

26 June Defiance Campaign begins in Johannesburg and Port Elizabeth. Over 8 000 people from all race groups court imprisonment by contravening selected discriminatory laws and regulations.

June Native Laws Amendment Act.
July Natives (Abolition of Passes and Coordination of Documents) Act.

August Mandela & Tambo law firm is established in Chancellor House, opposite the magistrate's courts in downtown Johannesburg.

remove this threat before the next poll in 1953, but stripping the coloureds of their vote took five years, and one reckless measure after the next.

The 1951 Separate Representation of Voters Act, which the NP submitted separately to the Assembly and the Senate, winning each by a simple majority to avoid having to gain the two-thirds majority from both houses sitting together as laid down in the Constitution, was dismissed in a unanimous Appeal Court decision. The government then created a parliamentary committee of MPs, called the High Court of Parliament, with powers to overrule Appeal Court decisions on government legislation. Again, this was defeated in the courts. But the Nationalists bounced back, passing yet another law to enlarge the Appeal Court bench – and appointing new judges favourable to the cause – and, for good measure, enlarging the Senate in such a way that guaranteed the party's dominance.

* * *

If this was a time when, as historian William Beinart said of the 1948 election, 'white politics mattered deeply', it was the gradual surge of black political activism in shantytown and rural kraal that made apartheid an increasingly controversial and beleaguered proposition. There was resistance from whites, too, and the beginnings of international opposition. South Africa's strategic significance to the Western Atlantic world – as guardian of the Cape sea route and as an exporter of important minerals – earned it a measure of toleration from Britain and America.

But the start of decolonisation across Asia and Africa brought new voices to international affairs, which proved discomforting to a South Africa intent on bucking the global trend of enfranchisement and liberation. The United Nations' first decision, sponsored by the government of India at the moment of its independence from Britain and Empire in 1947, focused criticism on South Africa's treatment of Indian citizens (a Smuts law to limit their property ownership rights), and elevated the international profile of the country's racial politics.

All black people living in 'white' South Africa had to carry a pass, and produce it on request, or face imprisonment. Over the years, hundreds of thousands were jailed as a consequence of this inflexible regulation.

August Security police conduct unprecedented raids on the offices and homes of the liberation movements and their leaders.

12 August Twenty leaders are arrested and charged under the Suppression of Communism Act, including James Moroka, Walter Sisulu, president of the South African Indian Congress Yusuf Dadoo, and ANC Youth League president Nelson Mandela.

12 September Thirteen Asian and Arab states ask the UN to consider the question of race conflict in South Africa arising from apartheid.

18 September Minister of Justice CR Swart tells Parliament 33 trade union officials and 89 others have been served with notices in terms of the Suppression of Communism Act.

October Nelson Mandela is elected president of the Transvaal ANC to replace the banned JB Marks.

8 November Police fire on demonstrators in Kimberley: 14 killed and 39 wounded.

At home, ex-servicemen who had so recently joined in the fight against fascism abroad were successfully mobilised in the early 1950s in Torch Commando protests in the major cities against the government's protracted campaign to remove coloureds from the common voters' roll. The campaign, led by Second World War fighter pilot Group Captain Adolph 'Sailor' Malan, was supported by some 250 000 war veterans at its height, and had its bloody moments.

At the end of May 1951, Cape Town's Groote Schuur Hospital was filled with dozens of injured men and women after a clash with police left shop windows smashed and the railings torn from the courtyard of the Groote Kerk in Adderley Street. Police said they were attacked with bottles and stones and scorched by the marchers' signature flaming torches, but the protesters said police had charged 'without restraint'. In heated exchanges in Parliament the next day, acting United Party leader Harry Lawrence warned the government that 'something bubbled over' in the protest which had been too long suppressed and who could tell what the position would be in ten years if timely steps were not taken. Angrily, a Nationalist MP shot back: 'You will be hanged!'

But the protest fizzled out eventually, weakened by its leaders' failure to take a clear position on black rights, or to allow coloured ex-servicemen to join its ranks. Confidence was no doubt drained by the consolidation of Nationalist power in the 1953 election – still winning on a minority of white votes, as in 1948, but gaining another 34 seats. It was later suggested that the main weakness of the flaring of white opposition in the Torch Commando was that it failed to develop a programme with the express objective of taking political power.

Lasting white opposition continued in different forms. Divisions in the increasingly ineffectual United Party led to the Progressive Party breakaway that would eventually become the main liberal opposition to the National Party. Outside Parliament, the Black Sash, a white women's group formed at the time of the constitutional protests, sustained a politics of conscience, switching its attention in due course to passes, influx control and forced removals. The Black Sash would later observe of the gathering force of apartheid that 'there is no record of even chattel slavery anywhere having produced so impossible a social situation – such a zoological experiment with human beings is historically unprecedented'.

---

10 November One-day general strike held in Port Elizabeth to protest police attacks in Kimberley and East London.

12 November Chief Albert Luthuli is dismissed as a traditional chief by the government after he refuses to resign as ANC leader in Natal.

2 December The trial of 20 national leaders comes to an end when they are convicted of 'statutory communism' and sentenced to nine months' imprisonment with hard labour. However, the sentences are suspended for two years.

But it was the shift in the sentiments and the tactics of black political organisations that did most to embattle white nationalism and transform the character of apartheid politics. For a long time, courtesy and moderation had been the main features of black South Africa's attempts to get whites to think differently about the rights of the majority, but the polite letters and the appeals to reason and a sense of fairness fell mostly on deaf ears, or were spurned. Albert Luthuli, elected leader of the African National Congress (ANC) in 1952, acknowledged that, at the end of the 1940s, it 'did not seem of much importance whether the whites gave us more Smuts or switched to Malan. Our lot had grown steadily worse, and no election seemed likely to alter the direction in which we were being forced.' But growing frustration among younger activists at the failure of leaders of the ANC to check the erosion of black rights in the 1930s and early 1940s generated a fresh, militant outlook, signalled in the Cape by the formation of the Non-European Unity Movement and, in Johannesburg, the ANC Youth League under Anton Lembede. Prominent members included young lawyers Nelson Mandela and Oliver Tambo and unionist Walter Sisulu.

While the ANC itself had grown its membership and branches under the direction of medical doctor Alfred Xuma, elected leader in 1940, and made rejection of discrimination its guiding principle, by the end of the decade it was the Youth League's more aggressive Programme of Action that was adopted by the movement. Key Youth League members – such as Mandela – gained influential positions in the leadership. This was a clear break from the ANC's more conciliatory stance of earlier decades. The Youth League's plan – inspired by the huge mineworkers' strike of 1946 and the resolve of wartime Johannesburg squatter movements – made 'national freedom' its central objective, and called for mass action, such as civil disobedience, boycotts and strikes, to achieve it.

To start with, Lembede, Mandela and others believed that the oppression of black people was a challenge for blacks to confront on their own, and they rejected collaboration with the Communists or coloured and Indian organisations. But under the influence of Xuma's successors, James Moroka and Luthuli, who were convinced of the virtue of united action, the Youth League leaders changed their minds. Members of the Communist Party had already proved their worth as theorists, organisers and outspoken activists. Similar political talent and

---

5 December UN sets up a Commission on the Racial Situation in South Africa

8 December Patrick Duncan and other whites illegally enter black locations in support of the Defiance Campaign.

December ANC elects Albert Luthuli as president-general to replace James Moroka.

1953

Government announces the Native Labour (Settlement of Disputes) Act in an attempt to control the trade unions.

Hendrik Verwoerd, the National Party's indefatigable theorist, proved himself undaunted by the task of charting the destiny of South Africa's 'Native' majority.

determination was present in coloured and Indian organisations. Joined together, the ANC leadership recognised, the broader front of resistance to apartheid would be stronger.

In passing the Suppression of Communism Act in 1950 – outlawing the Communist Party and making it harder for its members to participate in efforts to check apartheid – the Nationalists were no less mindful of the risks of a united front. This law was among the conditions that helped guarantee it. The scene was set for an escalation of the contest.

* * *

The year 1952 stands out in the decade as the counterpoint to 1948. Where, in the second election of the 1940s, the Afrikaner nationalists seemed to come from nowhere to grasp power, so just four years later their extra-parliamentary opponents formed up to strike a blow at white illusions about the powerlessness, or insignificance, of black people. Popularly called the Defiance Campaign, the Campaign for the Repeal of Discriminatory Legislation was planned jointly by the ANC and the South African Indian Congress in 1951, with a launch date of 26 June – Freedom Day – the next year. The strategy was simple but effective, non-violent but disruptive: volunteers would deliberately break discriminatory laws, compelling the police to arrest them. Mandela – who had risen rapidly in the ranks, and was elected as Luthuli's deputy in 1952 – would be the volunteer-in-chief.

The timing of the protest was powerfully symbolic, coming at the tail end of white South Africa's celebrating the 300th anniversary of the arrival at the Cape of the first permanent European settlers under Jan van Riebeeck. On 4 April, in one of the final events of the celebrations, a three-mile-long pageant weaved its way through central Cape Town. A crowd of some 45 000 turned out to watch and wave flags, packing the pavements and the balconies and windows of taller buildings.

First three tribal authorities established in the Transvaal.

Former Communist Party of South Africa (CPSA) members reconstitute the party as the South African Communist Party (SACP) at an underground conference.

March Public Safety Act and Criminal Law Amendment Act.
April Bantu Education Act.

'Many of the hundreds of horses in the parade, untrained to crowds, showed signs of nervousness, and only expert handling kept them under control,' a news report said. 'At the top of Adderley Street the crowd surged back when a span of oxen started running, and the voorloper had to lean back on his heels to stop them.'

No such handy evasive action was available to the authorities to bring black defiance to heel. At about the same time as the crowd-pulling pageant in Cape Town, James Moroka told a crowd of 50 000 people gathered at Freedom Square in Fordsburg that 'whites … cannot escape the fact that whatever page they turn in the history of South Africa they find it red with the blood of the fallen, with ill-will and insecurity'. The government warned ANC leaders that it would 'use the full machinery at its disposal to quell any disturbances', but – as the ANC had intended – there were, to start with anyway, no disturbances to speak of; the defiance was orderly and non-violent, and police were left with little choice but to do exactly as the volunteers meant them to do and that was arrest them.

By April 1952 the government's programme had entered a new, far-reaching phase. After the relative uncertainty of quite how to proceed in making the apartheid idea meaningful, but also practical, in the country's day-to-day social and economic life, the rise of Hendrik Frensch Verwoerd was significant. The brilliant former academic and newspaper editor felt wasted in the Senate, to which he had been appointed in 1948 after failing to gain a seat in the Assembly. Young NP colleagues – among them PW Botha, later the finger-wagging State President of the 'Fortress Apartheid' years – agreed, believing that the clear-minded, ideologically keen Verwoerd was the man to shape the future. Historian Robert Ross said of the Dutch-born Nationalist that he was a man 'of domineering intellect, contemptuous of fools and opponents, categories he tended to conflate'. Verwoerd himself once remarked that he had never experienced the anxiety of thinking that he might perhaps be wrong.

Having long believed there had to be a comprehensive, consistent plan rather than piecemeal dabbling where circumstances permitted it, Verwoerd brought his large-canvas thinking to bear when appointed Minister of Native Affairs in 1950. His promotion made him the overlord of the country's 10 million black people – nearly 70% of the population – and he moved rapidly to apply his thinking to ordering their fate.

April National Party wins its second general election.
24 April Albert Luthuli calls off the Defiance Campaign.

May Liberal Party is formed.
15 August Cape ANC leader Professor ZK Matthews proposes a Congress of the People.

September Coloured People's Organisation, later the Coloured People's Congress, under the presidency of James La Guma, is formed in Cape Town as successor to the African People's Organisation (APO).

His key instrument, introduced in 1951, was the Bantu Authorities Act, which abolished the Natives' Representative Council, the last pretence of black representation in mainstream white-dominated politics (which the ANC had abandoned anyway in the late 1940s), and created in its place the administrative architecture for homeland or Bantustan administrations – tribal, regional and territorial authorities in the reserves. These were not to be elected, but appointed by the minister of a department soon meaningfully named 'Bantu Administration and Development'. Verwoerd detested the term 'Native' for blacks, preferring the catch-all term 'Bantu' to convey the ethnic distinctiveness this determined sociologist constantly drew on in his theoretical justifications of 'separate development'.

A year later, he introduced the deceivingly named Natives (Abolition of Passes and Coordination of Documents) Act, which brought into a single so-called reference book every black person over 16 had to carry at all times a host of identifying details, from fingerprints and Population Registration card to signatures of employers and entries relating to labour bureaus and influx control.

Simultaneously, the Native Laws Amendment Act limited access to, and movement between, towns and cities. No black person could stay in an urban area for longer than 72 hours without a permit unless he had been born and was permanently resident there. Work seekers were compelled to use labour bureaus. The idea was to limit the black presence in urban areas to people who were working in the 'white economy' and, in the long term, to create a migratory labour system that would draw on black workers living in homeland reserves. In time, hundreds of thousands of people would be 'endorsed out' of towns and cities for not meeting legislative requirements. Families were broken up, and poverty, insecurity and hopelessness stalked those who didn't match Verwoerd's ideal.

Broadly, his goal was to reverse the core process of South African history – the movement of people from countryside to town and city and the growing interdependence of urban life. He hoped that he could at once diffuse black nationalism by rekindling tribal identities, and gain an acceptance of Afrikaner nationalism by convincing black people to 'go home' to their rural places and emulate it through their restored tribal authorities and what he supposed was their traditional way of life. In this way, black and white destinies could be separated and, as he

October Congress of Democrats is formed.
October Reservation of Separate Amenities Act.
December ANC adopts a proposal to call a Congress of the People.

30 December UN rejects South Africa's claim that it has no competence to adopt a resolution on apartheid, by 42 to 8 votes with 10 abstentions.

1954

South African Coloured People's Organisation organises bus boycott in Cape Town to protest against the introduction of segregation on buses.

saw it, inevitable racial competition and friction steadily reduced by providing a framework in which black political and economic aspirations could be satisfied without threatening white survival. It represented a massive disruption of black lives.

Mounting pressure on black communities deepened the spirit of resistance, spurring the growth of opposition and of the broad front of the ANC. 'The unity of Africans, Indians and coloured people,' Mandela observed during the Defiance Campaign, 'has now become a living reality.' In all, more than 7 500 volunteers were arrested before the campaign was called off, chiefly because of sporadic outbreaks of violence in clashes with police. To some extent, the campaign may have played into the Nationalists' hands, giving them a ready excuse to ban and arrest black leaders, and to introduce harsher legislation to curb opposition; the Criminal Law Amendment Act of 1953 prescribed severe penalties for anyone breaking a law as an act of political protest. The spectre of black muscle-flexing also stimulated white anxiety, driving up support for the NP in the 1953 ballot.

But the Defiance Campaign had its spinoffs for the Nationalists' opponents, too; it proved the effectiveness of non-violent mass action, and it hugely expanded the profile of the ANC. Between 1951 and 1953, the movement's paid-up membership climbed from 7 000 to 100 000, and its network of branches grew from 14 to 87. While opposition to apartheid was increasingly frustrated by the government's banning or 'restricting' leaders – Luthuli and Mandela were among them – the net effect, more than weakening resistance, was greater organisational effectiveness, in part by compelling activists to function increasingly in underground mode.

* * *

By the mid-1950s, apartheid's legal framework was complex and comprehensive. At work and play, South Africans were divided by the scrupulous observation of an anachronistic distinction between 'Europeans' and 'Non-Europeans'. If the 'imponderable force of custom' – as the communist and former MP Brian Bunting described the habitual ways of society – had long defined racial separateness in South African life, the 1953 Reservation of Separate Amenities Act enforced it by regulation. It was applied to trains and buses, beaches, park benches, pubs and

---

Federation of South African Women is formed. Regional and local conferences held to collect demands to be included in the Freedom Charter.

Oliver Tambo is banned and forbidden to address or attend gatherings.
Joint Planning Committee, later renamed the National Action Council, is established to organise the Congress of the People.

1 August Natives Resettlement Act allows the government to remove Africans from any area in the Johannesburg district. The objective is to clear Sophiatown.

post office entrances, restaurants, cinemas, public toilets, camping sites, or any other public facility. This became known as 'petty' apartheid.

Implementing the grand design – the wholesale separation of populations – was held up or muddled by the labour needs of the economy and the pragmatic course the government was compelled to follow to keep factories and farms going, and growing. But Verwoerd never took his eye off the big picture, and worked away assiduously, introducing measures in 1953 and 1954 which would deeply affect socio-economic outcomes well after the abandonment of apartheid.

The Bantu Education Act of 1953 took control of black schooling away from provinces and placed it in the hands of Verwoerd's Department of Bantu Administration and Development, all but breaking the influence of the 5 000-odd mission or church schools, which had long produced confident, articulate and politically conscious black graduates, and establishing a pattern of black education that was deliberately inadequate to modern social and economic aspirations.

Verwoerd couldn't have been crisper in defining his intent when he said his policy was that

> Bantu education should stand with both feet in the reserves and have its roots in the spirit and being of Bantu society … There is no place for [the Bantu] in the European community above the level of certain forms of labour … What is the use of teaching the Bantu child mathematics when it cannot use it in practice? That is quite absurd. Education must train people in accordance with their opportunities in life, according to the sphere in which they live.

This 'sphere' was given sharper definition in 1954 when the Native Resettlement Act made its way through Parliament to equip the Nationalists with a legislative wedge to prise existing communities apart.

Even as apartheid was being fashioned, there were signal instances of mixed suburbs clinging to a semblance of normal city life, not without squalor or grime, but with a spiritedness that was perhaps only next encountered in the 'New South Africa' of the 1990s. Johannesburg's Sophiatown, once called the 'Chicago of South Africa', was such a place, bohemian almost, as popular among writers and musicians as gangsters and small-time rogues. Developed initially

---

2 December JG Strijdom succeeds DF Malan as Prime Minister.

1955
Government announces that black women must carry passes.

Black Labour (Settlement of Disputes) Amendment Act.

Pupils from a nearby Indian school demonstrate their loyalty to
Congress leaders in a 1955 protest at Freedom Square in Fordsburg.

as a white suburb by a land speculator in the closing years of the 19th century, it had, by the 1950s, developed a distinctive and lively character not least as the home of African jazz and dance styles – kwela and mbaqanga, and the energetic tsaba-tsaba dance – that made Aunt Babe's, The Back of the Moon and other shebeens a magnet for homegrown talents.

The melting-pot suburb's infectious and defiant cultural energy was intolerable to Verwoerd and he was determined to destroy it; the Native Resettlement Act was designed for this purpose, though slum clearance and the provision of better basic housing for the poor were its pretexts. There were protests, but none strong enough to resist.

A newspaper report of early 1955 contains a striking image of Verwoerd's fastidious interest in the practical application of his intellectual vision. On the morning of 9 February, while 2 000 armed police stood by as the Natives Resettlement Board 'began moving the first batch of 150 Native families from the buffer strip in Sophiatown to their new Government-built homes in Meadowlands' nearly 20km away, Verwoerd 'sat beside a telephone in Cape Town and was given reports of the move every half an hour'. These bulletins must have left him feeling content:

> As the Natives moved out of their homes and rooms in the pouring rain, anti-rodent squads from the city health department moved in with cyanide gas pumps and when they had finished, gangs of Native wreckers took over and demolished the shanties.
>
> There was no violence and no resistance by any of the families, who were removed with their goods on three-ton army lorries. Most of them said that they were glad to move, but several said their only worry concerned the new rents and the cost of travelling to their work from Meadowlands. White bread was handed out to each family at 9.30 a.m. when the first truck reached Meadowlands, one loaf for every three people. Cool drinks were given to each Native and before the truck moved on to the allotted houses, a dustbin was handed to each family. Then they were shown round their new homes and every piece of furniture was unloaded and put in place.

The new costs, the distances to workplaces, the helplessness in the face of armed police and unmoved officials – and, for a while, the bread-and-cooldrink illusion of passive black contentment – would be the recurring themes of apartheid

Black Sash is formed by six women in Cape Town.
Tomlinson Commission report calls for a massive job creation programme in the reserves.

9 February Start of removal of about 60 000 people from Johannesburg's Western Areas, including Sophiatown.

April Government assumes control of 'Bantu' schools.

Police monitor the removal of the first 60 Sophiatown families (above), whose belongings were heaped on trucks bound for Meadowlands. Spare, uniform housing in the new township (right) awaited the thousands evicted from 'white' Johannesburg.

social engineering. Eventually, more than 60 000 people were moved to Meadowlands in the emerging complex of Soweto, the vast dormitory settlements of the South Western Townships on the fringe of Johannesburg. Verwoerd had the satisfaction later on – it took years to complete the clearance – of seeing bulldozers flattening what once was Sophiatown, and in its place a newly built suburb, for whites, being named Triomf (triumph).

In the years to come, many of the giants of South African music – among them Miriam Makeba, Hugh Masekela, Dollar Brand (Abdullah Ibrahim) and Letta Mbulu – eventually left the country to pursue their careers abroad, memories of the vibrance of old Sophiatown venues becoming poignant tokens of a greater loss. Yet, as historian Luli Callinicos notes in *The World that Made Mandela* (2008),

> if apartheid's social engineers thought they would crush the vitality and creative resourcefulness of black culture by removing Sophiatown's black residents to Meadowlands, they were mistaken … Over the years [the neighbourhoods] bonded to form well-knit, supportive communities. Burial societies, cooperative savings clubs – known as 'stokvels' – women's charity groups, choirs and dance, theatre and music clubs all flourished throughout the apartheid years. The members of the Soweto String Quartet, to name just one well-known group, were born and bred in Meadowlands.

25 & 26 June About 8 000 delegates representing the ANC, the Congress of Democrats, the South African Indian Congress, the Coloured People's Congress and the multiracial South African Congress of Trade Unions meet at Kliptown, near Soweto, in a Congress of the People. The Freedom Charter is adopted.
July Criminal Procedure Act.

September Homes of all prominent protest leaders are searched for incriminating evidence.

The outspoken Anglican priest Trevor Huddleston, a Sophiatown resident himself, acknowledged at the time that there was nothing especially lovely about Sophiatown in its material decrepitude, and that in contrast Meadowlands 'is a pleasant site … [a]nd if you are used to locations, I suppose it bears comparison with any other … [being] at least just as dull'. But the uprooting of its people made him weep, he said, because it was 'being carried out with the connivance of the Christian conscience of Johannesburg' and that 'in spite of all we have tried to do, we have failed so utterly to uphold principle against prejudice, the rights of persons against the claims of power'.

Where Verwoerd persisted, in his dispassionate academic way, in casting apartheid as a scheme that held just as much social, economic and political benefit for black South Africans as it did for whites – if only they'd see the sense of it and go along with 'separate development' in the tribal reserves – his Prime Minister, JG Strijdom, DF Malan's successor, dispensed with the politesse in a 1955 speech in Parliament that spelled out clearer than ever what apartheid was about.

> *Call it paramountcy, baasskap or what you will, it is still domination. I am being as blunt as I can. I am making no excuses. Either the White man dominates or the Black takes over … The only way the Europeans can maintain supremacy is by domination … And the only way they can maintain domination is by withholding the vote from non-Europeans … The government of the country is in the hands of the White man and for that reason the White man is baas in South Africa.*

The simple premise of white domination would last for decades, but it gave way eventually to the principles which in that same year of 1955 were drawn up in a charter fashioned by an assembly of 2 884 like-minded black, coloured and Indian activists, and a few white liberals, communists and churchmen, at a dusty sports ground near Soweto. The government hoped it had broken the organisational reach of opposition outside Parliament by banning scores of ANC, Indian Congress and trade union leaders in 1953 in the aftermath of the Defiance Campaign. But the gathering of delegates from all over the country at Kliptown in June 1955 proved the Congress movement was more resilient than that.

The idea of a positive declaration of intent for the opposition was first raised by the academic and influential ANC thinker ZK Matthews in 1953, and for two

Miriam Makeba and the Manhattan Brothers – South Africa's acknowledged 'Kings of Song' – typified the creative vitality of Sophiatown's music and dance scene.

27 October 2 000 women, of all races, march in Pretoria coordinated by the Federation of South African Women over the lack of social services, housing and schools and the threat of the extension of passes to women.

December Lillian Ngoyi becomes the first woman to be elected to the ANC's national executive committee, at the national conference in Bloemfontein. Africanists at the conference attack the Freedom Charter's commitment to multiracialism.

years volunteers criss-crossed the country, visiting villages and townships, farms and factories, churches and sports clubs, to find out what the people wanted their future to be. The Congress of the People at Kliptown was the culmination, the proceedings being witnessed by some 7 000 spectators – many carrying placards such as 'Votes for All', 'Freedom of Speech', 'Down with Passes' and 'Down with Bantu Education' – as well as a contingent of armed police. By the time the police acted, wading into the crowds to take down names and confiscate documents, it was too late; the Congress had already delivered the Freedom Charter – asserting rights to equality without consideration of colour, race, sex or belief within a democratic state based on a universal franchise – that would guide the struggle for years to come, providing its resounding slogan, 'The people shall govern.'

The opening line of the Charter was a direct challenge to the Nationalists' determination to dominate: 'We, the people of South Africa, declare for all our country and the world to know … [t]hat South Africa belongs to all who live in it, black and white, and that no government can justly claim authority unless it is based on the will of the people.'

'Nothing in the history of the liberatory movement,' Albert Luthuli said of Kliptown, 'quite caught the popular imagination as this did, not even the Defiance Campaign. Even remote rural areas were aware of the significance of what was going on.' So was the National Party. The show of democratic rather than just demonstrative resolve at Kliptown was the prelude to the next phase of the contest in which two courtroom dramas – the indecisive Treason Trial and, less than a decade later, the critical Rivonia Trial – gave sharper definition to the shift from protest against discrimination to the struggle for freedom.

* * *

On that May morning in 1948 when Mandela and Tambo had stopped to take in the headlines announcing the NP's election victory, Tambo, much to Mandela's surprise, expressed some satisfaction at the result. 'I like this,' Mandela recalled his saying. 'Now we will know exactly who our enemies are and where we stand.' Certainly, by 1955, the schism couldn't have been clearer. The question was, who would gain the upper hand, and how? The forces facing each other across an increasingly divided landscape were uneven, but the starker the choices became, the less the scope for deferring action. The same was true for both sides.

Sophiatown residents turn out in force in February 1955 in the vain hope of stalling their eviction under the government's Native Resettlement Act.

CHAPTER TWO

Trial of will

1956-64

Nelson Mandela wears an expression of resolve in this
November 1958 photograph – taken when the state's
case against the Treason Trialists was faltering – as
if he foresaw that even if the prosecution failed, as it
did in 1961, the Nationalists would not give up. Behind
him, to his right, is his young wife, Winnie.

In the second week of February 1956, women of the Black Sash set out in their cars from towns and cities across the country in a road show of sorts that would culminate in Cape Town in a last effort to oppose the government's dogged five-year struggle to strip coloureds from the common voters' roll. V-for-victory signs, thumbs-up salutes and warm congratulations, occasionally offset by taunts such as 'vuilgoed' (rubbish), greeted the doughty women as they crossed the hinterland. On the whole, they received more approval than they'd expected.

'At some Karoo towns,' said Mrs Ruth Foley, national president of the Women's Defence of the Constitution League, 'we were wished well by people who could scarcely speak English.' The same was not true for Mrs MM Hitchman of Kimberley who, while resting at a hotel in Worcester, was accosted by a man who said bluntly: 'We would like to push you into the sea.'

But these women were equal to such threats, convinced as they were about just how much was at stake. In one Orange Free State car was a party from the Welkom branch of the Black Sash, driven by Mr PJ Pienaar, whose wife had persuaded him to drive them down. 'We are an old Free State family,' Mrs Pienaar told a reporter. 'Our people came up with the Voortrekkers. I feel deeply religious about this; I feel we are in danger of losing something we may never recover.' And yet, perhaps, the loss was already irrecoverable.

Almost exactly a week earlier, the *Cape Argus* newspaper said in an editorial:

By the time these words appear in print, the joint sitting will doubtless be nearing its end, and the Separate Representation of Voters Act will have been validated by the two-thirds majority artificially contrived for the purpose … What has happened to-day is not a beginning but an end. It is the end of faith in the White man's word, the end of the entrenched sections, the end of the aspirations towards unity based on the agreement of Union. Henceforth, South Africa will live, but with honour tarnished. Every promise made by the White man to the non-European or by one White section to the other will, in future, be read in the light of the pledges given in 1931 and 1936 and scattered to the winds to-day.

1956

2 March South Africa Act Amendment Act.
16 March Riotous Assemblies Act.
31 March and 1 April ANC formally adopts the Freedom Charter at a special conference, despite disruptions by Africanists.

18 May Separate Representation of Voters Act finally removes coloureds from voters' roll.
1 June Native Administration Amendment Act empowers the government to banish Africans to remote rural areas.

9 August Women march to the Union Buildings in Pretoria, under the banner of the Federation of South African Women, to protest against the pass law.

All that remained to be done was for the government to pass the South Africa Act Amendment Bill to revalidate the earlier, twice-defeated Separate Representation of Voters law. On the very day of the Black Sash women's cross-country trek to the Cape from the Welkoms and Kimberleys of the north, the hubbub in Parliament reflected a rampant National Party's assurance of being able to steamroller its opposition, the House of Assembly 'packed as never before' for the formal notice of motion of the new legislation. 'There are so many Senators now,' a news report said, 'that more than 40 of them have to be accommodated in the benches beyond the bar of the House, from which Senators usually watch proceedings in the Assembly in their spare time.'

Looking back, it is possible to say of the late 1950s and early 1960s that while even the most assured, and certainly the thinking, Nationalists knew that every step they took from here on would be resisted by opponents too numerous

In deliberately solemn ranks, women of the Black Sash stand in silence outside the Johannesburg City Hall to 'mourn' the failure of constitutionalism in the government's stubborn effort to strip coloured people in the Cape of their voting rights.

5 December Police arrest 156 leaders of the Congress Movement.
19 December Preliminary hearings begin in what will become known as the Treason Trial.

1957

Immorality Amendment Act declares sex between whites and blacks 'immoral'.
Transkeian Territorial Authority replaces the Bunga and takes on limited government responsibilities.

South African Congress of Trade Unions organises major workers' strikes and actions around the country.
April South African Coloured People's Organisation rejects the Separate Representation of Voters Act.

merely to push into the sea, the white opposition of Hitchmans and Pienaars who drew on the values of English liberalism, or of sincere and, in a certain light, even progressive Great Trek pragmatism, would dwindle. The deeper apartheid went, the deeper and more natural-seeming, or habitual, became the schism between black and white.

* * *

By 1956, black South Africa's faith in the power of non-violent mass action – the strategic vehicle of the 1952 Defiance Campaign – was intact, but strained. The bannings and restrictions imposed on leaders from 1953, and the scant impact of protests on an indifferent and implacable government, which had only increased the penalties for resisting, suggested there was little future in the strategy. It was still, at least, a means of registering mass opposition, impressively illustrated in the gathering of 20 000 women in the pass protest mounted by the Federation of South African Women outside the Union Buildings in Pretoria in August 1956. But, with the Freedom Charter now in place as the lodestar of a collective avowedly non-racial effort at confronting discrimination, the peaceful disobedience inspired by the Indian hero Mahatma Gandhi was beginning to seem too tame a response to apartheid. As it happened, it was the government that paved the way to the decisive shift in the way in which apartheid would be fought.

Having confiscated heaps of documents from the Kliptown gathering in June the previous year, investigators spent all of 1956 poring over what they believed amounted to evidence of insurrectionary plotting. The length of time spent formulating their case suggests the government was determined to chronically weaken, if not destroy, their opposition once and for all by isolating all the key leaders and jailing them. This much began to emerge at dawn on 5 December 1956 when, in what newspapers referred to as a 'Union-wide swoop', police arrested 140 people in all the major centres, descending on homes in suburbs and townships at 5am to net the activists whom the government regarded as their greatest threat. Some of them, forty years later, would have the satisfaction of voting the principal tenets of the Freedom Charter into being in a democratic constitutional state founded on a Bill of Rights. Back in 1956, however, such unprejudiced conviction amounted to treachery.

Women from all communities of the Witwatersrand converged on the Union Buildings (opposite) in October 1955 to reject Bantu Education legislation and plans to extend passes to all blacks. The march was a precursor to the 20 000-strong women's anti-pass protest in Pretoria on 9 August 1956,

17 December After almost a year of preliminary hearings, the government drops charges against 61 of the Treason Trial accused, including Albert Luthuli and Oliver Tambo.

1958
All African men are required to carry reference books.
17 March ANC is banned in several rural districts.

3 April Coloureds elect four whites to the House of Assembly in the first communal election since their removal from the common voters' roll in 1956.
16 April National Party wins its third election.
24 August Prime Minister JG Strijdom dies.

The placards, and the public support, left the government in little doubt about popular loyalty to the anti-apartheid struggle when the preparatory examination of the 156 Treason Trialists got under way in Johannesburg at the end of 1956.

It was all very dramatic. In the Cape and Natal, after brief appearances before specially convened magistrate's courts, the arrested leaders were bundled into military aircraft and flown to Johannesburg. Among them was the MP and resident of Cape Town's affluent suburb of Clifton, LB Lee-Warden, the Native Representative for the Western Cape. Aside from the big names, such as Albert Luthuli, ZK Matthews, Nelson Mandela, Walter Sisulu, Oliver Tambo and Helen Joseph, there were scores of others not widely known to the general public at that time. Charges were eventually brought against 156 people from all of apartheid's neatly partitioned 'population groups' – 105 blacks, 23 whites, 21 Indians and seven coloureds.

Police held warrants to gather up yet more piles of evidence – documents and articles, account books, financial returns, letters, minute books, draft speeches,

3 **September** Dr HF Verwoerd becomes Prime Minister and leader of the National Party.
November Africanists break away from the ANC.
8 **December** All African People's Conference is held in Accra, Ghana.

1959
4 **April** Pan Africanist Congress is formed under the leadership of Robert Sobukwe.

June Promotion of Bantu Self-Government Act and Extension of University Education Act passed by Parliament.
July PAC leader Robert Sobukwe announces plans for a campaign against pass laws.

cablegrams, diaries, membership cards, lectures, films, shorthand notes and even typewriters and recording machines.

The range of organisations whose leaders or members were arrested reflects the wide front of resistance, from the African National Congress, South African Indian Congress, South African Coloured People's Organisation and the mostly white Congress of Democrats to 'non-European' youth movements, the Springbok Legion, the South African Society for Peace and Friendship with the Soviet Union, the World Peace Council and its South African associates, the Congress of the People, the Communist Party, the Federation of South African Women, the Congress of Trade Unions, the World Federation of Trade Unions, the Friends of China Society and the Western Areas Protest Committee. Collectively, they amounted to what *Drum* magazine journalist Anthony Sampson described at the time as 'South Africa's real opposition'.

Just 14 days later, in a specially constituted court in Johannesburg's Drill Hall, the preliminaries of South Africa's biggest trial got under way. In the hours before the hearing was to start, a crowd of 300 supporters stretching around three sides of the Drill Hall swelled to more than 5 000, with men and women parading around the block in twos and threes in sandwich boards reading 'We stand by our leaders.' But would the leaders and their organisations survive the onslaught the government was intent on delivering at this juncture?

*   *   *

In the second half of the 1950s, the Nationalists had every reason to feel flushed with success. They had finally succeeded in removing coloured voters from the common roll and now had crammed every major opponent into the dock in the Treason Trial. Apartheid was becoming an increasingly accepted, even ordinary, idea, the observance of which, despite continual controversy and moral criticism, was assuming more and more the character of custom, seemingly just a stricter or starker version of the segregation that preceded it.

In June 1959, for instance, students and principal at the University of Cape Town 'clashed again' on the issue of mixed dancing at campus events, the University Council incensing the student body by insisting that 'in non-academic or social matters, such as dances, it is most desirable ... that the university abide by

November Liberal-minded members of the United Party break away to form the Progressive Party.
16 December ANC's last national conference before its banning.

1960

24 January Cato Manor riots in Durban result in the deaths of nine policemen.
February Rebellion in Pondoland prompts Luthuli to warn whites that black resentment is mounting.

3 February British Prime Minister Harold Macmillan delivers his 'wind of change' speech in Parliament.
March ANC announces that its anti-pass campaign will start at the end of March.

By any sporting definition, Sewsunker 'Papwa' Sewgolum was a star, but in apartheid South Africa the two-time Dutch Open champion was so disadvantaged he was tempted to give up golf altogether.

the customs and conventions of the community in which it exists'. A dance attended by 'whites and non-whites … is definitely … against the best interests of the university'.

Early in 1961, twice Dutch Open golf champion and holder of the South African non-European golf title, Sewsunker 'Papwa' Sewgolum, was actually thinking of giving up golf altogether because 'there does not seem to be any future for me here any more.' He couldn't play in the Natal Open, he said, 'and it is quite likely that I won't be allowed to play in the South African Open'. Two years later, when golf champions were entertained to a cocktail party and braaivleis at the river resort of Maselspoort, near Bloemfontein, it was reported that the two honoured 'non-whites', Sewgolum and Ismael Chowglay, would be entertained separately, in a garage.

Neither university life nor the game of golf suffered anything like terminal disruption on account of such 'normal' racial aberrations.

For all the cross reaction in Parliament and elsewhere in 1957 to Prime Minister JG Strijdom's summary institution of 'Die Stem' as the sole national anthem – prompting accusations that he had 'insulted' English-speaking South Africans, 'perpetuating hatreds' by disregarding their sentiments – the Nationalists' gains in the general election of April 1958 reflected widening white support for apartheid. The NP won its third consecutive election with the largest majority yet, claiming 103 seats to the UP's 53, and, for the first time since 1948, a majority of votes. It was an election of which one newspaper noted: 'The appeal to race and to fear has won again … Capital outflow, job reservation, burdensome legislations, rising costs of living, increasing isolation, the enlarged Senate, swollen taxation, the monstrous growth of bureaucracy and the rejection of total apartheid have not weighed in the balance at all. Fear of the non-White and chiefly of the Native has been decisive.' The National Party – especially under the new Prime Minister Hendrik Verwoerd, who took the reins after Strijdom died in office in 1958 – would not have wanted it any other way.

A year later, there were signs that the ruling party's opposition both in and outside Parliament was breaking up when 12 liberal-minded MPs left the United

21 March Police open fire on pass protesters in Sharpeville, killing 69. Protests spread, and a state of emergency is declared in 80 magisterial districts. The armed forces are put on alert. Verwoerd tells Parliament that the riots are not a reaction against apartheid but a 'periodic phenomenon'.

27 March Pass laws are briefly suspended (until April 6).

28 March Oliver Tambo leaves South Africa illegally on the instructions of the ANC to carry on its work outside the country. Albert Luthuli is detained and held until August,

when he is tried, fined £100 and given a six-month suspended sentence.

1 April UN Security Council, in its first action on South Africa, deplores police action in the country and calls for the abandonment of apartheid.

Party to form the Progressive Party, and 300 members of the ANC broke away under Robert Sobukwe to form the Pan Africanist Congress (PAC). The United Party splintered over the search for a more progressive path towards white South Africa's accepting the idea that the country belonged to all. The schism in black politics arose over differences on whether centuries of colonial dispossession by whites could adequately be overcome by the Freedom Charter's assertion that South Africa did, indeed, belong to all.

Claims that Africa belonged to Africans were stimulated across the continent when, in the glare of a battery of floodlights at a polo ground in Accra at midnight on 7 March 1957, Dr Kwame Nkrumah proclaimed Ghana's freedom and independence to a crowd of 30 000 ecstatic citizens. Nkrumah and his fellow Cabinet ministers all wore white skullcaps bearing the magic letters PG, the badge of those jailed for political activities and therefore entitled to call themselves 'prison graduates' – a detail in newspaper reports of the time that would resonate throughout Africa's shift to independence, though not for South Africans for more than three decades.

In contrast to the tantalising fact of Ghana's statehood, Nationalist-led South Africa was intent on devising a different future based on a different kind of belonging. This was given more concrete form in the late 1950s with Verwoerd's

ANC leader Chief Albert Luthuli with lawyer Oliver Tambo (above, left), who became the standard-bearer of the outlawed liberation movement over three decades of exile from the early 1960s. Robert Sobukwe (above, right) led the 1959 breakaway from the ANC to form the Pan Africanist Congress (PAC).

7 April Under the Unlawful Organisations Act, the ANC and PAC are banned for a minimum of one year. Only the four Native Representatives and members of the Progressive Party vote against the law.

9 April Attempted assassination of Verwoerd at the Rand Easter Show by a white farmer described as mentally unstable.

May/June First boycotts of South African goods begin in many countries.

4 May Sobukwe is sentenced to three years' imprisonment for incitement. He refuses to appeal, and refuses the aid of an attorney, on the grounds that the court has no jurisdiction over him because it cannot be considered either a court of law or a court of justice.

ascendance to the prime ministership, a position of authority he used to drive what became the homelands – or Bantustan – policy, the broad-canvas 'solution' to southern Africa's political destiny.

Public debate about making grand apartheid workable was significantly influenced by the findings of a commission headed by agricultural economist Professor FR Tomlinson. The commission had been appointed in 1949 by DF Malan; by the time it had completed its work in the mid-1950s, Verwoerd, by then the NP's unassailable theorist in chief, was confident enough in his own thinking about southern Africa's future to reject much of its substance. The Tomlinson report in essence called for massive investment in the homeland regions to make them economically viable, and for the consolidation of some 260 scattered reserves into seven tribal blocks.

While Verwoerd was not prepared to spend huge sums on the reserves, or see more white farmland given over to consolidating them, the Tomlinson report must have seemed, to those who wished it to be, a corroboration of the principle of black people pursuing their civic and economic aspirations in their 'own' areas, leaving the bulk of the country to whites. The gist, again, was the trusty notion of future security: 'The policy of separate development,' Tomlinson wrote, 'is the only means by which the Europeans can ensure their future unfettered existence …'

But where Tomlinson, whose demographic projections showed continued and substantial black populations in urban areas, predicated his ideas on massive investment in rural areas to offset urbanisation, Verwoerd's thinking rested on using law and regulation to force a separation of interests. The glaring inequity in the fact that the tribal lands reserved for 70% of the population accounted for a mere 13% of the country left Verwoerd undaunted.

His first measure as prime minister, the 1959 Promotion of Bantu Self-Government Bill, imposed eight homeland authorities on the affairs of the 260 scattered reserves, authorities beholden to the government through its appointment of chiefs and headmen. Verwoerd stripped blacks of their limited representation in Parliament (by seven white MPs), offering that if the administrations of the 'Bantustans' – as they almost immediately came to be known – proved themselves capable of it, full independence was a possibility in a distant future

---

6 May Parliament is told 18 000 people have been detained since the proclamation of the emergency. The emergency is lifted on 31 August.

June Representation of blacks in Parliament ends.
5 October Whites vote in a referendum in favour of establishing a republic.

1961

23 January UN secretary-general Dag Hammarskjöld announces that, in discussions with Verwoerd, 'so far no mutually acceptable arrangement' has been found on South Africa's racial policies.

in which white South Africa could conceivably be the central, guardian state of a regional commonwealth.

Verwoerd's administration also deepened the reach of its exclusionary education policy for black people in 1959 with the perversely named Extension of University Education Act, closing existing English-language universities to black students, and providing for 'ethnic colleges' in the Bantustans. Among the statements of protest against this law was a warning from the University of the Witwatersrand that if 'native' medical students were barred from its medical school, the effect would be that only one black doctor for every million black people would be trained in future.

By 1960, the scaffolding, if not quite the edifice, of grand apartheid was taking form in an atmosphere dimmed by the foreboding shadow of the Treason Trial. This was the setting, as the new decade opened, for the somewhat inauspicious state visit by British Prime Minister Harold Macmillan, who felt compelled to tell

University of the Witwatersrand students protest against the Extension of University Education Act, which denied black students access to established campuses, and provided for 'ethnic colleges' in the Bantustans.

26 February Government announces that existing defence relations with the United Kingdom will continue.

12 March International Confederation of Free Trade Unions calls on the UN to endorse economic sanctions against South Africa.

15 March South Africa withdraws from the Commonwealth. The Synod of the Dutch Reformed Church expresses support for the policy of apartheid. Professor AS Geyser, who questions whether discrimination is in line with the Scriptures, is bitterly attacked.

29 March Treason Trial ends with the acquittal of the remaining 30 accused. Hours later, the ban on the ANC and PAC is renewed for another year.

South Africa that Britain didn't like apartheid much and that it ran counter to the surely irresistible political currents of the time, a force he memorably characterised as a 'wind of change'. The gathering shift to independence in Africa begun in Ghana in 1957 would continue through the 1960s as former colonies gained self-rule.

When, on 2 February 1960, Macmillan addressed MPs and senators in the dining-room of Parliament, he might have sounded encouraging to his predominantly Nationalist audience when he condemned attempts in Britain to organise a boycott of South African goods as undesirable from every point of view – 'Boycotts will never get you anywhere.' But his speech is remembered chiefly for what he said next:

> [I]t is our earnest desire to give South Africa our support and encouragement, but I hope you won't mind my saying frankly that there are some aspects of your policies which make it impossible for us to do this without being false to our own deep convictions … We ought, as friends, to face together, without seeking to apportion credit or blame, the fact that … this difference of outlook lies between us.

Macmillan's reasoning made little impact on Verwoerd's stony conviction. In his long discussions with the South African Prime Minister, Macmillan later recalled,

> I began to realise to the full extent the degree of obstinacy, amounting really to fanaticism, which he brought to the consideration of his policies. Even in small matters he had pressed apartheid to its extreme. In a country where there is at least the advantage of being able to enlist African staff, he refused to have a single African in his house. An old and rather incompetent Dutch butler looked after us. The Prime Minister, with his quiet voice, would expound his views without any gesture or emotion. At first I mistook this calm and measured tone for a willingness to enter into sincere discussion. However, I had the unusual experience of soon noticing that nothing one could say could have the smallest effect upon this determined man.

British High Commissioner Sir John Maud later wrote that when Macmillan asked about the position of the 11 million black people living in the 87% of the Union reserved for three million whites, Verwoerd's answer was unhesitating: 'Like Italians working as miners outside Italy, they will have no political rights outside the homelands; their position will be that of honoured guests.'

---

5 April Britain votes for a UN resolution against apartheid for the first time. On 13 April, the UN declares apartheid 'reprehensible and repugnant to human dignity' in a 95-1 vote.

29 May Nationwide general strike.
30 May Union of South Africa officially ceases to exist at midnight. The Republic of South Africa comes into being. CR Swart is sworn in as the first president.

26 June While underground, Nelson Mandela writes a letter in which he states: 'The struggle is my life. I will continue fighting for freedom until the end of my days.'

Verwoerd's grand planning, though, ran counter to the thrust of post-war history and the expectations that went with it, and was especially prone to accidents of fate. A little more than a month after Macmillan's portentous address in Cape Town, the headline news from South Africa told of the killing of 69 people in a pass protest at Sharpeville. The country, and apartheid itself, had reached a critical juncture.

The Sharpeville massacre, as it came to be called – though it was almost certainly the result of the panicked reaction of scared and poorly led police – occurred on the first day of a protest called by the newly formed Pan Africanist Congress. Earlier, the ANC had announced plans for a pass protest at the end of March; keen to upstage its bigger rival and, presumably, demonstrate the scale of its support, the PAC set the date for its own protest ten days sooner.

The killing by police of 69 pass protesters at Sharpeville on 21 March 1960 was a turning point; resistance on all fronts stiffened, and the first seeds of doubt were planted in the Nationalist mind.

18 October National Party achieves gains of 10% in a general election. Helen Suzman enters Parliament.

20 October All meetings to protest against arrest, trial or conviction of any person are banned.

December Pamphlets are distributed by ANC armed wing, Umkhonto we Sizwe (Spear of the Nation), announcing new methods of struggle.

A schoolboy, Philip Kgosana, led this protest march into central Cape Town in 1960, bringing home to a complacent establishment the anger inflamed by the Sharpeville massacre.

The atmosphere was tense as protesters gathered at the police station at Sharpeville on the morning of 21 March. The slogan that drove the demonstration was 'No bail, no defence, no fine', and so they waited, determined to have themselves arrested. Sabre fighter jets ordered to fly low over crowds here and elsewhere had succeeded in dispersing some protesters, but nobody budged at Sharpeville.

In the early afternoon, after police reinforcements had been brought in and the crowd lining the perimeter fence of the police station had swelled to some 5 000, a scuffle near one of the gates and a surge in the crowd triggered the tragedy; without warning, police opened fire, even as people fled. Most of the 69 dead and 200 wounded were shot in the back. There were violent confrontations in Langa in Cape Town, and elsewhere too.

Across the country, and the world, condemnation was swift. But so was the reaction of the government. In declaring a state of emergency, cancelling all police and army leave, arresting some 18 000 people, and hastily passing laws to ban the PAC and the ANC, it displayed only stubborn indifference. The PAC's leader, Robert Sobukwe, was immediately arrested, and jailed on Robben Island. (After six years there, he was released into house arrest at his home in Kimberley,

11 December Albert Luthuli receives the Nobel Peace Prize in Oslo. He says: 'I regard this as a tribute to Mother Africa, to all peoples, whatever their race, colour or creed.'

16 December Formation of Umkhonto we Sizwe, to 'hit back by all means within our power in defence of our people, our future and our freedom'. There is a strict undertaking that life will not be endangered, and only installations will be attacked.

A central high command, with regional commands, is set up under the direction of Mandela. Five bomb explosions occur in Johannesburg and five in Port Elizabeth.

where he remained under a banning order until his death in 1978.) Economic confidence dipped as investors and many in the white business community began to have doubts about their prospects.

Jitters grew when, just three weeks after Sharpeville, Verwoerd was shot in the head at point-blank range by a deranged white farmer. He survived, but his absence while recuperating was grasped by Nationalist thinkers who, fearing a widening uprising, growing international isolation and further economic decline, openly expressed their misgivings about apartheid in its rigid Verwoerdian mould and suggested the party consider offering a 'new deal' of some kind to black people. Acting Prime Minister Paul Sauer – whose report in the mid-1940s had underpinned the electorally decisive concept of 'apartheid' as a governing policy – could not have been bolder in expressing these misgivings when he declared in a constituency speech that 'the old book of South African history was closed' and that the whole question of race policy should be reconsidered in a spirit of inter-racial trust so that black people could be given a sense of hope 'and not feel that they are continually being oppressed'.

In fact, Sauer stopped far short of contemplating meaningful political rights for blacks. Even so, this was a moment when the country might have taken a different route. It's imponderable whether, in the absence of Verwoerd, a National Party that seemed to be having second thoughts would have found it possible to begin feeling its way towards a new departure, some sort of rapprochement with the likes at least of Albert Luthuli, whose stature as a leader of the African cause – and a Nobel Peace Prize winner in 1961 – was matched by his commitment to a negotiated solution.

Only days after the Sharpeville killings, Luthuli, giving evidence in the Treason Trial, which was still lumbering along four years after it began in 1956, foresaw conditions in which, as a result of strikes and demonstrations, the white public would 'from sheer self-interest … persuade the Government to enter into negotiations with us to see if our demands can be accommodated'. But any such possibility – even the tinkering reforms suggested by his Acting Prime Minister – was scotched by Verwoerd himself. In a statement read to Parliament on his behalf in May, he said dismissively: 'One must guard against the tendencies among some people to see the disturbances in the wrong perspective, and

1962

January Mandela secretly leaves the country to attend a Pan African Freedom Movement conference in Addis Ababa; he travels to other countries to receive military training, and meet political leaders, before returning to continue operating underground.

23 January Verwoerd announces plans to grant 'self-rule' to the Transkei.

29 March Defence minister JJ Fouché discloses that South Africa is buying supersonic Mirage III jet fighters from France, and that South African forces are being equipped with French Alouette helicopters.

April 1961 protesters in London's Oxford Street count Hendrik Verwoerd's walkout from the Commonwealth a victory for apartheid South Africa's isolation. Oliver Tambo, third from the left, became a key figure in sustaining international pressure on apartheid.

against the agendas of opponents to try to use the events and the atmosphere to encourage a revision of policy … The government sees no reason to depart from the policy of separate development.'

When, later in the year, Verwoerd returned to work, fully recovered, he was, as journalist Brian Lapping noted, 'treated with the adulation due to one risen from the dead'. Yet, in his reaction to Sharpeville, and to the wiser Nationalists, like Sauer, who had begun to question race policy, he generated the strife succeeding governments would have to contend with for the next three decades.

Such a future was crisply defined by one of the women of the Black Sash who, four years earlier, had tried vainly to influence white opinion against scrapping coloured political rights in the Cape; at the end of March 1960, Ruth Noel Robb warned in a letter to a newspaper that 'to banish the leaders or to ban the

17 May Dr Jan Steytler, leader of the Progressive Party, launches a nationwide protest campaign against the General Laws Amendment Bill, which defines the crime of sabotage in the widest terms.

27 June Parliament passes the General Law Amendment Act
5 August Nelson Mandela is arrested near Pietermaritzburg. He is sentenced to five years' imprisonment on 7 November.

7 September South African Congress of Democrats is banned.
13 October First restrictions to house arrest under the Sabotage Act are imposed in Johannesburg on Helen Joseph.

organisations will be to lose the power of negotiating and possibly to send the two main movements underground. If that were to happen we should all of us be living in a state of siege in our own country.'

Verwoerd, however, was wholly undeterred, pressing on towards the end of 1960 with his plan for a referendum among whites on whether the Union should become a republic and once and for all sever its historical ties with Britain. Whites were fairly evenly divided on this, but on the day an early anti-republican lead was steadily whittled down. There was some robust rivalry as the two sides rallied supporters; at a polling station at Retreat in Cape Town a republican stuck his head into an anti-republican car and shouted abuse at the women passengers only to have a custard tart plastered all over his face. Evidently anticipating more than an electoral challenge, anti-republican campaigners at a polling station in Johannesburg secured the services of a heavyweight wrestler and four ducktails to guard their tent. In the end, though, custard pie and brawn were not enough to staunch the go-it-alone sentiment of the 850 000 republicans who won the referendum with a majority of 74 000 votes.

In mid-March 1961, the final communiqué from the Commonwealth conference in London announced South Africa's withdrawal from the club of former empire states two and a half months before it was to become a republic. The country's departure followed a vain 15-hour debate on trying to reconcile Verwoerd's views with those of the other ten Commonwealth heads of government at the conference. There was no meeting of minds in what one newspaper described as a 'quarrel unprecedented in the history of the Commonwealth'.

Back home, anxiety over the implications for the one thing that white South Africa treasured more than most – rugby – was dispelled by South African Rugby Board president Danie Craven, who said defiantly: 'I don't expect any trouble ever over future tours.' The sporting fraternity's confidence was misplaced. South Africa was soon turfed out of the Olympic movement, its participation in the 1960 Rome Games being the last for decades, and, though it took time to develop, 'trouble' over future tours was assured by growing sporting isolation.

The end of March 1961 brought a more immediate setback for the government. The Treason Trial, South Africa's largest and longest, which had sought to find 156 leaders of the most significant opposition organisations guilty of

10 December Albert Luthuli and Dr Martin Luther King, Jr, issue a joint statement, 'Appeal for Action Against Apartheid'.
21 December International Court of Justice at The Hague rules by a narrow majority (eight votes to seven) that it has jurisdiction in the case brought by Ethiopia and Liberia alleging that South Africa had violated its mandate over South West Africa.

1963

14 March Publications and Entertainment Act controls importation, distribution, exhibition, sale or possession of any publications deemed 'undesirable'.

A characteristically dapper Nelson Mandela chats with fellow ANC Youth League leader Peter Nthite in a lunch break during the Treason Trial.

being communists – a crime under apartheid – and of plotting to overthrow the state by force, drew to a close in a humiliating defeat.

The prosecution of the first charge in particular had been so inept that after several months of embarrassment the state dropped all charges against 65 of the accused and limited the case against the remaining 91 to treason. By the end of March 1961, charges had been dropped against all but 30 of the original 156, and even against these the judges found the state had failed to prove its case. All were acquitted. It was a signal moment in the conduct of politics in South Africa. As Sharpeville had compelled the liberation movements to shift their focus from protest to liberation, the failure of the Treason Trial and, with it, the idea of trying to use the courts to impose its will convinced the government to rely instead on developing a repressive security apparatus.

One man who saw all too clearly the true meaning of the trialists' triumph was Nelson Mandela. He wrote much later that he did not regard the verdict 'as a vindication of the legal system or evidence that a black man could get a fair trial in a white man's court', arguing that the doubtless 'just verdict … was largely as a result of a superior defence team and the fair-mindedness of the panel of these particular judges.' Mandela went on:

> After more than four years in court and dozens of prosecutors, thousands of documents and tens of thousands of pages of testimony, the state had failed in its mission. The verdict was an embarrassment to the government, both at home and abroad. Yet the result only made the state more bitter towards us. The lesson they took away was not that we had legitimate grievances, but that they needed to be far more ruthless.

Mandela had emerged during the trial as a figure of growing importance. In his testimony he demonstrated the combination of resolve and democratic conviction for which he would later be fêted – gratefully embraced, almost – by

May Security police begin 90-day arrests. A widespread purge of 'subversive elements' is undertaken.

1 May Justice minister John Vorster announces that Robert Sobukwe has been taken to Robben Island where he will be detained indefinitely in terms of the General Law Amendment Act.

11 July Senior ANC leadership arrested at Liliesleaf Farm, Rivonia.

18 July UN Special Committee on Apartheid recommends an effective embargo on exports of arms and ammunition and petroleum to South Africa.

most white South Africans. His undertaking in a statement during the trial to 'force the whites by using our numbers ... to grant us what we demand' might not have seemed to the ruling minority in the early 1960s to square with his view that this 'is not a direct threat to Europeans' since the Congress 'has consistently preached a policy of race harmony and we have condemned racialism no matter by whom it is professed.' But it was on the strength of such testimony that the three judges concluded unanimously that the state had failed to prove that its opponents were bent on violent change as a matter of policy.

Ironically, perhaps, in the weeks after the conclusion of the trial, Mandela grasped the challenge of forging a new kind of campaign, the armed struggle. There did not seem to be any other option. Before the government could re-arrest him, Mandela slipped underground to begin reorienting black opposition. While on the run in June 1961, he issued a statement that defined the future and provided iconic rhetoric for later generations of activists.

Treason Trialists – Nelson Mandela, right, among them – are bused from Johannesburg to Pretoria for another day in court.

I have chosen this course ... to live as an outlaw in my own land ... I shall fight the government side by side with you, inch by inch and mile by mile, until victory is won ... Only through hardship, sacrifice and militant action can freedom be won. The struggle is my life. I will continue fighting for freedom until the end of my days.

Oliver Tambo later said of him: 'Of all that group of young men, Mandela and his close friend and co-leader Walter Sisulu were perhaps the fastest to get to grips with the harsh realities of the African struggle against the most powerful adversary in Africa.' Tambo himself had to contend with a costly feature of this harsh reality when he was sent abroad with the objective of developing an international dimension to the struggle. The PAC, not as successfully, was compelled to do the same, establishing a presence in Maseru and elsewhere in Africa.

International support was significant; the founding of the Anti-Apartheid Movement in 1959 and the Treason Trial Defence Fund – forerunner of the

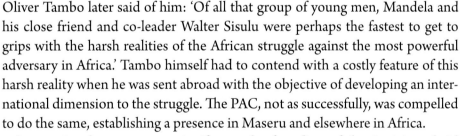

11 August Harold Wolpe (arrested on the Bechuanaland border) and Arthur Goldreich (arrested in the Rivonia raid) escape from the Johannesburg Central Police station, and on 28 August emerge in Bechuanaland.

9 October Rivonia trialists – Walter Sisulu, Nelson Mandela, Govan Mbeki, Ahmed Kathrada, Rusty Bernstein, Dennis Goldberg, James Kantor, Andrew Mlangeni, Elias Motsoaledi and Raymond Mhlaba - charged with sabotage and attempting to overthrow the state. The trial begins on 3 December.

In the Cape, the trial begins of members of the Non-European Unity Movement - Neville Alexander, Don Davis, Marcus Solomons, Elizabeth van der Heyden, Fikile Bam, Ian Leslie van den Heyden, Lionel Davis, Dorothy Alexander, Dulcie September, Doris van der Heyden and Gordon Hendricks.

Defence and Aid Fund which, for the next three decades, would play a key role in assisting apartheid's opponents – helped to keep 'the Pretoria regime' in a spotlight of controversy. The United Nations (UN) called for a voluntary arms embargo against South Africa in 1963, and a year later recommended economic sanctions as a means of bringing apartheid to its knees. But for all the media attention, and the condemnation of apartheid by foreign governments and organisations such as the UN, the Non-Aligned Movement and the Commonwealth, sustaining the international arm of the struggle was a long, lonely effort.

The government was confident of being able to check resistance. Mainly as a result of the harsh post-Sharpeville crackdown – against what Verwoerd characterised as 'a few trouble-makers' – protests had largely died down. After the failure of the Treason Trial, however, the risks of newly emboldened opposition prompted the Prime Minister to stiffen the fight in a way that meant he wouldn't have to depend on the courts. To this end, he appointed former Ossewabrandwag firebrand and wartime internee John Balthazar Vorster as his Minister of Justice. Vorster famously recalled telling Verwoerd that 'you could not fight communism with the Queensberry Rules,' to which the premier had replied that 'he would leave me free to do what I had to do – within reason'. This was dangerous latitude.

When, at the end of 1961, just a week after Albert Luthuli's return from being awarded the Nobel Peace Prize in Oslo, the government's confidence was rocked by a series of bomb blasts organised by the ANC's newly formed armed wing, Umkhonto we Sizwe, Vorster acted as he believed the circumstances required.

The government's answer to the 18-month bombing campaign was steadily longer periods of detention without trial, solitary confinement, summary banishment through house arrest, more brutal methods of interrogation, and, in 1963, a so-called Sabotage Act that provided for a definition that went far beyond the ordinary meaning of 'sabotage', along with harsh penalties equivalent to those for treason.

Mandela and other key figures in the founding of Umkhonto we Sizwe – 'Spear of the Nation', or MK, as it came to be known – had always expressly insisted that the armed struggle would be limited to sabotage, not killing or injuring people. In the government's mind – and probably much of white South Africa's – the distinction was slim. And perhaps understandably, considering the militant tone

20 **November** First elections to the 45 seats for elected members of the Transkei Legislative Assembly take place. There are no political parties, the choice being between candidates supporting Chief

Kaiser Matanzima and those supporting Paramount Chief Victor Polo Ndamase of the West Pondos. They are outnumbered by 64 appointed chiefs. On 11 December, Chief Matanzima is installed as chief minister.

1964

17 **January** Leader of the opposition, Sir De Villiers Graaff, demands judicial inquiry into the activities of the Broederbond, and demands the Prime Minister resign from it. Verwoerd refuses.

of the leaflet announcing MK's formation: 'The time comes in the life of any nation when there remain only two choices: submit or fight. That time has now come to South Africa. We shall not submit and we have no choice but to hit back by all means within our power in defence of our people, our future and our freedom …'

If apartheid was morally condemned by the repression that sustained it, the struggle would also have to contend with the moral stresses brought by its shift to militancy and methods of violence. But as the avenues for peaceful resistance closed and the indifference of most of white society deepened, the options available to the cause of national liberation narrowed. As Mandela said later, 'we had either to accept inferiority or fight against it by violence.'

South Africa was, by the 1960s, a society defined by divisions former MP Brian Bunting described as a combination of 'impenetrable legal barriers, physical distance and the imponderable force of custom'. To the atmosphere of anxiety associated with the penalties for opposing apartheid and the growing climate of secrecy that obscured the government's widening repertoire of repressive techniques were added deliberate measures, such as the Publications and Entertainments Act of 1963, to limit society's exposure to challenging opinions or alternative visions of social modernity. Even mildly progressive views or images fell foul of the law; all appearances of black American jazz virtuoso Louis Armstrong were excised from the film *The Glenn Miller Story*, and, in the poster for *Ocean's 11*, showing Sammy Davis, Jr, walking down the street side by side with Frank Sinatra, Dean Martin and Peter Lawford, the outline of Davis was turned into a featureless black shape. Among banned books were *I, Claudius* by Robert Graves and an account of the life of Marilyn Monroe. The press attracted increasing hostility, even where it merely reflected actual political conditions; English-language newspapers were

Sabotage of installations such as power lines marked the start of the armed struggle against apartheid by Umkhonto we Sizwe (MK) and the African Resistance Movement.

28 February Draft Bill proposes a Coloured Representative Council.

7 March Minister of Posts and Telegraphs, Dr Albert Hertzog, rules out television for South African audiences.

21 March National budget for 1964/65 provides for R210 million on defence, an increase of R52 million over the previous year, in order to 'discourage foreign aggression', according to Defence minister Eben Dönges.

18 April Neville Alexander and four others are found guilty of sabotage and sentenced to ten years' imprisonment.

Kaizer Matanzima, later the strongman of Transkei, doffs his hat as he greets a senior police officer during an official engagement, a gesture of deference his critics would have said typified his relationship with apartheid South Africa.

accused on one occasion of being complicit to 'sabotage and crime'.

In 1962, when the outspoken liberal Helen Suzman entered Parliament for the first of her 13 years as the sole representative of the Progressive Party – a token in itself of the political complacency of the bulk of white society – she noted: 'I am ... the only person in this House apparently who belongs to a party that does not have to indulge in *swart gevaar* [black menace] tactics ... It seems to me that my party is the only party in this country [apart from the unrepresented Liberal Party] which does not shake with fear at the implications of accepting South Africa as what it is, and that ... is a multi-racial country.'

Under such conditions, a militant underground resistance was inevitable, but it took skill and energy to fashion, and Nelson Mandela was among those who gave it his untiring attention. Having become an 'outlaw in my own land', he crisscrossed the country, organising defiantly and deftly evading the police, earning himself the moniker of the 'black pimpernel'. In 1962, he travelled abroad, first to a number of African states (he received some military training in Algeria), and then to Britain, where he hoped to gain support for the ANC's armed wing, and a sympathetic understanding of the change in the movement's strategy.

Soon after returning home, while driving to Natal to meet Albert Luthuli and brief him on his travels, Mandela's car was stopped near Howick and he was arrested. He had been on the run for more than a year. The government, conscious of the risks of being outmanoeuvred, had devoted considerable resources to developing a network of paid informers. It was clear that, for a fee, someone in the know had tipped off the police about Mandela's movements. The charges brought against him – inciting people to strike and leaving the country without a passport – were enough to earn a five-year prison term, the heaviest sentence yet imposed in apartheid South Africa for a political offence. John Vorster's police, and their paid informers, would soon have a great deal more to crow about.

20 April UN Group of Experts on Apartheid recommends that 'all the people of South Africa should be brought into consultation and should thus be enabled to decide the future of their country at the national level'.

16 May Commission of Inquiry into the South African Press tables its report, severely criticising newspaper reporting and recommending a press council to control newspapers and correspondents.

23 May Albert Luthuli's first five-year ban expires, but he is immediately served with a new and stricter order.

To the heavy legislative programme of 1963, Verwoerd had the pleasure of adding the Transkei Constitution Act, a key step in validating the grand plan of satellite Bantustans. The Transkei, the largest and most developed of the tribal reserves, was an obvious choice for making a start on getting a significant portion of the black population onto a 'self-governing' footing.

An important ally in the process was former minor chief Kaizer Matanzima who, in the first elections for the Transkei Legislative Assembly in 1963, garnered most of his support from chiefs paid and appointed by the government, while his main rival, Paramount Chief Victor Poto – who favoured the Transkei's remaining an integral part of a single, united South Africa – attracted the bulk of support from elected members. Later indications of wider backing for Matanzima prompted the *Rand Daily Mail* newspaper to observe, of the Nationalists' interpretation that this meant growing black support for apartheid, that 'this is, of course, bunkum. Africans do not support apartheid. They may accept it as an unpleasant fact which they are powerless to change, and make what adjustments they can the better to live with it. But they do not support it; no people anywhere have ever supported a system of oppression against themselves.'

Central to the delusion of political independence in the Bantustans was that the white economy depended on black – and much of it migrant – labour, and the homeland economies depended on income earned in the white-controlled towns and cities and on farms. It was all carefully managed to ensure that economic interdependence didn't neutralise the political vision of separate interests and, chiefly, white supremacy. In this, the Native Laws Amendment Act of the early 1950s was a devastating blow, enabling government officials to 'endorse out' – effectively 'repatriate' to homeland areas – black people who did not have the necessary permits to work in the urban areas. It was revealed in Parliament that between 1956 and 1963 more than 464 700 black people had been 'endorsed out' of 23 major towns and cities. It often meant husbands were separated from wives, parents from children. 'The real cost,' the Black Sash noted, 'must be counted in terms of human sorrow, bitterness, suffering and tragedy on a vast scale.'

Under such conditions, political activism mounted, but so did state repression, illustrated by the fact that between March 1963 and August the next year,

---

9 June UN Security Council urges South Africa to end the Rivonia Trial and grant an amnesty to all detained or banned opponents of apartheid.

12 June All but one of the Rivonia trialists – Rusty Bernstein – are sentenced to life imprisonment.

13 June In terms of a new General Law Amendment Act, the death penalty is extended to people who have undergone sabotage training within South Africa.

Liliesleaf Farm in Rivonia is deceptively placid in this contemporary aerial photograph of the scene of the dramatic arrests of the main leaders of the ANC's underground formations.

there were 111 political trials in which 1 315 people faced charges relating to their political activity. Forty-four of them were sentenced to death, and 12 to life imprisonment. By the admission of Commissioner of Prisons General JC Steyn himself, there were about 8 500 political prisoners in South Africa by 1965. The government dismissed objections to its use of torture and detention to halt opposition and armed resistance – the sabotage campaigns of MK and other smaller organisations, such as the National Liberation Front and the African Resistance Movement – arguing that its methods had proved effective.

The biggest catch came on the morning of 11 July 1963, when police – either through a tip-off from a former detainee or from intelligence gleaned by a secret agent who had infiltrated MK – raided a house at Liliesleaf Farm, Rivonia, outside Johannesburg, and netted the main leaders of the underground ANC and its armed wing. The arrested men included Walter Sisulu, Govan Mbeki, Raymond Mhlaba, Andrew Mlangeni, Ahmed Kathrada, Elias Motsoaledi, Dennis Goldberg and Rusty Bernstein. Nelson Mandela, who was already in prison, was flown to Pretoria and became Accused Number One in what came to be called the Rivonia Trial.

16 June Former Archibishop Joost de Blank presents a petition at the UN on behalf of the World Campaign for the Release of South African Political Prisoners (sponsored by the Anti-Apartheid Movement in London). The petition is signed by 91 691 people in 28 countries.

19 June Sabotage groups blast three electricity pylons, one in the Transvaal and two on the Cape Flats.

24 July A time bomb placed in the main concourse of the Johannesburg railway station explodes during the late afternoon, causing extensive injuries. John Harris is later tried and sentenced to death for this offence.

For seven months, the central contest of South African political life played out in the Palace of Justice in Pretoria, with the state determined this time to make the charges stick. Many Nationalists might have hoped the trial would end in death sentences. The trialists themselves feared the worst, and prepared themselves for it. At the close of his five-hour statement from the dock on 12 June 1964 – in the famous paragraph he had agonised over, and learned off by heart – Mandela provided the ongoing struggle against apartheid with its ringing clarion call:

> *During my lifetime, I have dedicated my life to this struggle of the African people. I have fought against white domination; I have fought against black domination. I have cherished the ideal of a democratic and free society in which all persons live together in harmony and with equal opportunities. It is an ideal which I hope to live for, and to see realised. But, My Lord, if needs be, it is an ideal for which I am prepared to die.*

In a sombre atmosphere three months into the Rivonia Trial, Albertina Sisulu (left, in traditional dress), Winnie Mandela (centre) and, behind her, Nelson Mandela's mother, Nosekeni, leave the Palace of Justice in Pretoria in December 1963.

The trialists were not hanged, but sentenced to life imprisonment, a fate the government anticipated would neutralise them and demoralise their supporters. However, even the headlines that day – 'Crowd sings as the sentences are known' was one – suggested otherwise. 'As soon as the sentences were heard,' the report said, 'a section of the crowd outside the court broke into song. Posters were unfolded, reading "We are proud of our leaders," "No tears will be shed," and "Sentence or no sentence we stand by our leaders."' A troop carrier full of armed policemen left the court in front of a truck carrying the convicted men to jail just before one o'clock. 'As the truck emerged the men pushed their hands out of the barred windows and gave the clenched fist sign. Hundreds of spectators, both Black and White, shouted in recognition.'

29 July Verwoerd rejects world pleas to reduce the sentences in the Rivonia Trial.

August Winnie Mandela and Albertina Sisulu are given permission to visit Robben Island, but are forbidden to travel together as they are both banned.

15 August Minister of Defence JJ Fouché announces that private enterprise will be responsible for the manufacture of aircraft for the South African Air Force. Jet trainers, to replace the SAAF's Harvards, will be the first aircraft to be made locally.

From London, newspaper readers learned of protests against the life sentences passed in the trial: 'A party of 60 students at Sussex University staged a protest march from Brighton to London last night and arrived early to-day, in spite of raging storms and torrential rain.' Among the marchers who had trudged through the night was the 21-year-old son of one of the accused, a man who would later lead a democratic South Africa into the 21st century before being forced out of office by his own party. His name was Thabo Mbeki.

Under cover of darkness, the Rivonia trialists were flown to Cape Town from Pretoria in a twin-engined Dakota, descending over a peninsula in whose wintry morning light Mandela remembers seeing 'the little matchbox houses of the Cape Flats, the gleaming towers of downtown … and out in Table Bay, in the dark blue waters of the Atlantic … the misty outline of Robben Island'. Here, a small, cramped cell 'was to be my home for I knew not how long'. It was a space he could cover in three steps, so confining that when he lay down, 'I could feel the wall with my feet and my head grazed the concrete on the other side.' A small eye-level window overlooked a courtyard.

But the 46-year-old prisoner drew on his own considerable mental stamina to preserve a greater view of his country and its future, an expansive vision which, after nearly three decades, would guarantee him a towering status as the almost uncannily unembittered leader of a democratic South Africa.

For prisoner 466/64 and the many others held at apartheid's Alcatraz, the 'long, lonely wasted years' were very hard. But for all the abuse, deprivation, fear and longing, the prisoners' fortitude and their conviction in the ideals which had cost them their freedom never dimmed. Mandela acknowledged later that, in the 1960s, the liberation movement had nurtured false hopes that the wind of change spoken of by Macmillan, which brought independence from colonial rule to African states, would prove irresistible in the south, too, delivering a non-racial democracy to South Africans at least within a decade.

But if the optimism in the liberation movement was unfounded, the government was just as wrong in thinking that jailing Mandela and others on Robben Island, banning their political organisations and turning the screws of repression would guarantee stability and acquiescence. At best, apartheid gained a false sense of imperviousness to a history largely of its own making.

---

24 September South African ordnance workshops produce the first Belgian FN rifle, which is now ready to go into production.

20 November Bram Fischer QC and 13 others, charged with being members of the banned Communist Party, go on trial.

10 December Verwoerd's Economic Advisory Council accepts a five-year plan to give South Africa an annual economic growth rate of 5.5%.

Above

This framed image at Robben Island shows Mandela in conversation with his long-time political companion and trusted confidant Walter Sisulu in the early years of their incarceration on the island

Right

For all its confining starkness, Nelson Mandela's Robben Island prison cell failed to deprive its famous inmate of his vision and optimism.

CHAPTER THREE

Fortress apartheid

1965-76

The sunny days of white South Africa's prosperous 1960s earned the Nationalists growing support, but Hendrik Verwoerd's determination to deepen rather than ease apartheid meant that the republic would soon begin to feel the heat.

U

nprecedented economic growth through the 1960s deepened South Africa's crisis even as it appeared to achieve the reverse. With resistance checked or obscured by an increasingly elaborate 'security' apparatus, the economic lurch of the post-Sharpeville crisis gave way to renewed investor confidence, on the strength partly of a period of high global economic growth, and of the profits to be made in an environment of plentiful cheap labour. Foreign investment of some R3 billion in 1963 rose to R7 billion by 1972, and the growth rate averaged 5.5% through the 1960s – when the young republic introduced its own currency, the rand – with imports and exports rising by more than 100%.

Among whites, better jobs and greater prosperity went hand in hand with a drop in the birth rate, rising car ownership – it had doubled every decade since 1940 – regular holidays and a secure suburban lifestyle. An Americanised consumerist culture took root. Looking back from the 1990s, the Reader's Digest *Illustrated History of South Africa* offered this memorable contrast:

> *An airline passenger travelling over Johannesburg's northern suburbs in the late 1960s could not have failed to notice scores of bright blue squares, ovals and rectangles dotting the spacious gardens of the homes hundreds of metres below him. The sight of so many swimming pools moved one observer, the writer Bill Johnson, to comment: 'At some point around 1970 white South Africans overtook Californians as the single most affluent group in the world.' However, had the plane swung towards Cape Town, a different sight would have greeted our traveller: south of the city, frequently hidden beneath a blanket of smog from thousands of wood stoves, lay Johannesburg's south-western townships (Soweto); ignored, silent, quiescent, smouldering. In a land of stark contrasts, this must surely have been the starkest of all.*

Stark it undoubtedly was, but for the enfranchised minority it was all but invisible. Growing international isolation matched a kind of domestic isolation too.

In *Twentieth-Century South Africa*, historian William Beinart writes: 'Most whites were unable to see black South Africans during this critical period in the

25 January Bram Fischer fails to arrive in court, forfeits his bail and goes underground. In a letter read to the court, he delivers a harsh attack on government policy.

12 February Group Areas Act proclamation reserves public places of recreation – sporting venues, theatres and concert halls – for one 'race' group or another.
18 March South Africa announces its first nuclear reactor has 'gone critical'.

7 April UN Special Committee on Apartheid is told of the execution of station bomber John Harris
13 May Official Secrets Act amendment prevents publication of information which could hamper the security police.

country's history. Homelands, passes, group areas, social amnesia, and powerful ideologies put them out of sight, literally and metaphorically. Whites believed they knew "their" Africans, and this justified their system against attacks from ignorant outsiders. Many of them came across Africans only as servants and workers.' South Africa seemed, to them, a success story and there was no reason to upset the status quo. English-speaking voters who had customarily opposed the Nationalists began to have a change of heart, largely because of the country's economic successes. In the 1966 election, the National Party was rewarded with

Leisure opportunities for whites matched their growing affluence in the 1960s, while blacks lucky enough to qualify as urban residents had to be content with waiting on the tables.

7 June Police Amendment Act, passed unopposed, empowers the police to search without a warrant any person or place within one mile of South Africa's borders and to seize anything found. It is designed to combat the infiltration of saboteurs.

4 September Verwoerd indicates that no Maoris will be acceptable in any New Zealand rugby team visiting South Africa in future.

27 October Verwoerd opens a new international radio service, 'The Voice of

South Africa', intended to counter hostile propaganda.

3 November Johannesburg Bar Council strikes Bram Fischer from the roll of advocates.

Helen Suzman, for 13 years the lone standard-bearer of liberalism in Parliament, addresses a Progressive Party rally in 1966.

a 21-seat gain from the United Party opposition – the biggest since 1953 – which gave it 126 of the 170 seats in the House of Assembly.

Two years later, the still lone standard-bearer of liberalism in Parliament, Helen Suzman, remarked that while

[A] lot of people pay lip service to this ideal of separate development … the vast majority … simply want the maintenance of the status quo. And that is, to put it quite bluntly, the maintenance of vast reservoirs of cheap black labour for the benefit of white employers in this country and the maintenance of white domination. That is all they want.

There was no doubt some truth in the comment in a newspaper report in the early 1960s by PW Botha, then Minister of Coloured Affairs, Community Development and Housing, that it was 'quite surprising to find that frequently individuals and institutions who fight tooth and nail against the Government's residential separation policy and shed venom on the Government for implementing it, in their own hearts wish it to be carried out'. Yet, as historian David Welsh notes, the idea among many whites that the peacefulness in society vindicated the removal of what were regarded as 'agitators and other subversives', and suggested black people were content, was deeply misleading. 'It was a profound misreading of black attitudes to suppose that sullen acquiescence equalled contentment. If anything, the apparent quiescence was the lull before the storm.'

1966

18 March Defence and Aid Fund is banned. Police search the homes of office-bearers, including that of writer Alan Paton.

30 March National Party wins a landslide election.

9 May Bram Fischer, rearrested in November 1965, is sentenced to life imprisonment.

4 June Senator Robert Kennedy visits South Africa as a guest of the National Union of South African Students. The government declines to meet him.

6 September Verwoerd is murdered in Parliament; succeeded by John Vorster.

27 September UN votes by 114 votes to two, with three abstentions, to end Pretoria's South West African mandate. South Africa ignores the decision.

The unforeseen results of the economic conditions of the time, coupled with the unintended consequences of more rigorously managed schooling for black children, and the creation of blacks-only universities, provided new focal points for resistance to apartheid.

The huge investment of foreign capital in manufacturing and commerce hastened structural change in the economy, with the contribution of agriculture and mining to GDP continuing to drop, and of services and manufacturing continuing to grow. These shifts brought changes to the workplace, and the workforce (skilled work grew, while unskilled labouring declined), giving black people – who accounted for more than two-thirds of the labour force by 1970 – new economic and political bargaining power.

The government's efforts to induce industry to relocate to the fringes of the Bantustans were less than successful. The so-called 'border industries' were intended to sustain homelands economically and staunch the migration of black labour to the cities, but economic growth depended rather on the factories and firms of the metropolitan centres. Even where job reservation was strengthened to protect white jobs and discourage black economic advancement in 'white' South Africa, regulations were eventually observed chiefly through the wholesale granting of exemptions to allow industry to employ black people – often to replace whites who, benefiting from the boom, were moving out of the blue-collar band.

All the while, despite the gross underfunding and inadequacy of Bantu education, black enrolment in schools rose steadily, going from 800 000 school places in 1953 to 1.8 million in 1963. Enrolment grew at an even faster rate through the rest of the 1960s, and with it the impact of widening literacy.

In the white community, younger people especially were responding to new influences chiefly brought or sponsored by consumerism, ranging from the anti-establishment sentiments of the Bob Dylans and Jimi Hendrixes of the hippie era to fashionable Marxist teaching at the universities to which a growing white middle class turned on its aspirant trajectory. Among younger Afrikaners, the hold of a traditional cultural identity was loosening as they felt the tugs of an alluring desire to be 'with it'.

Few of the implications of these dynamics were evident or were felt in any meaningful way until the first half of the 1970s.

1967

MK begins a joint campaign with ZAPU, a people's army fighting for the liberation of Zimbabwe, crossing the Zambezi River and entering Rhodesia's Wankie Game Reserve.

National Education Policy Act sets out the principles of Christian National Education for white schools.
19 April South Africa signs an agreement with France to buy Daphne-class submarines.

May Malawi's President Hastings Kamuzu Banda visits South Africa.
9 June Defence Amendment Bill, supported by the opposition, provides for compulsory military call-up for most young white men.

*   *   *

The conclusion of the Rivonia Trial in June 1964 was followed a month later by a bomb blast on the main concourse of the Johannesburg railway station – injuring 23, one fatally – which, rather than prompting second thoughts about apartheid, only helped to harden white attitudes. The bomber, 27-year-old schoolteacher John Harris, considered himself, in the phrasing of the 1980s, a conscientised South African. He was a member of a radical group in the Liberal Party, and, as chairman of the South African Non-Racial Olympic Committee, a key figure in assuring the country's exclusion from the Olympic fraternity. He joined the African Resistance Movement (ARM) and, just at the moment in 1964 when that organisation was broken apart by arrests and trials – in which the evidence of a former ARM detainee proved decisive – set his bomb. He insisted in his testimony that he had not intended to kill or hurt anyone, having telephoned a warning to the police and a newspaper some minutes before the blast. However, despite arguing that his bomb was akin to wartime sabotage by extreme anti-British Afrikaner groupings, Harris was sentenced to death. His wife, Ann, tried every avenue to save his life, including a direct appeal to an evidently unmoved Justice minister John Vorster. In a bid to rally public support, she organised a petition on Harris's behalf. It was signed by no more than 300 people. On 1 April 1965, he was hanged.

Another white man made headlines in 1964 when he was charged for his role in furthering the struggle as a committed member of the banned Communist Party. Bram Fischer skipped bail, worked underground for ten months, was rearrested and ultimately sentenced to life imprisonment. Fischer, Nelson Mandela's advocate during the Rivonia Trial, was a dangerous exemplar within Afrikanerdom; a respected advocate, he was also the scion of an esteemed Free State family, the grandson of a prime minister of the former Boer republic and son of the province's judge president. In a 21st birthday message, Ouma Steyn, widow of the last Free State president Marthinus Steyn, said of him: 'I know that Bram Fischer is going to play an honourable role in the history of South Africa.'

Such distinction counted little in the eyes of the court that tried him, and almost certainly counted against him in the Nationalist circles of the 1960s. Peers, too, turned their backs on him; the Johannesburg Bar Council struck

---

21 June Terrorism Act equates terrorism with treason. It is made retrospective to June 1962, and authorises indefinite detention without trial on the authority of any senior policeman, and makes information about detainees secret.

21 July Albert Luthuli dies. He is buried on 23 July.
30 July 'Luthuli Combat Detachment', comprising ZAPU and ANC guerrillas, crosses the Zambezi into Rhodesia at the start of the Wankie and Sipolilo campaign, which lasts until late 1968.

September Vorster launches his 'outward policy'.
23 September At a National Party rally, Vorster defends Pretoria's decision to send police to Rhodesia.

Fischer from the roll even before he was found guilty under laws promulgated by a government which, on the face of it, had little standing in a legal community that set much store by its rejection of injustice. In Mandela's estimation, by risking being ostracised by his own people Fischer had 'showed a level of courage and sacrifice that was in a class by itself'. It was certainly rare.

The Harris and Fischer cases earned extensive exposure, but were not by any means isolated instances of resistance ruthlessly crushed. Vorster's security police had infiltrated the underground formations of the Communist Party and the ANC and – often relying on the devastating evidence of detainees who had been turned through confinement and torture – all but neutralised them. Activists who were lucky enough to escape arrest fled the country to a life of hard, sometimes lonely and often debilitating exile.

But the struggle was not over. Fischer was no doubt correct when he warned his accusers: 'If today there is an appearance of calm, it is a false appearance induced entirely by … oppression … All it can achieve is a short-term period of quiet and long-term hatred.'

*   *   *

By a fateful convergence that had little, directly, to do with politics, establishment South Africa's sense of invulnerability was shaken when, on the afternoon of 6 September 1966, a mentally troubled parliamentary messenger made his way to the Assembly chamber at the start of the sitting. With a sheath knife concealed under his jacket, he approached the front bench, where an unsuspecting Prime Minister Hendrik Verwoerd sat impassively. Dimitri Tsafendas would later claim a worm in his stomach made him kill the premier, a motivation that earned him life-long detention as a madman.

In the very first press bulletin on the stabbing of the prime minister, the immediacy of present-tense reporting, rare in newspapers, seemed almost to preserve the possibility that Verwoerd might live: 'It is not yet known how seriously he is injured. He is slumped in his front bench, blood streaming from the wound. Members of Parliament who are doctors are attending him.' The bells signalling the start of the session were still ringing when Tsafendas made his way to the Nationalist leader's seat. Just as Verwoerd looked up as if he expected the

---

17 November Malawi announces details of its diplomatic arrangements with South Africa.
13 December UN's 21st session declares apartheid 'a crime against humanity'.

1968
5 April Defence minister PW Botha says countries inciting 'terrorism' against South Africa could provoke retaliation.
30 April The law establishing five universities for blacks takes effect.

4 May Armaments Development and Production Act establishes the Armaments Development and Production Corporation of South Africa (Armscor).
17 June UN says South West Africa shall henceforth be known as 'Namibia'.

Hendrik Verwoerd's bloodied body, draped in a sheet, is carried out of Parliament soon after his assassination by stabbing on 6 September 1966.

messenger was about to say something, Tsafendas suddenly drew his knife and plunged it into the Prime Minister's neck. Verwoerd did not live.

From a distance, it almost seems that the country – part of it, anyway – lost its head at this moment, grieving for a leader whose cold and single-minded brilliance had brought much grief to so many people. Verwoerd had no sooner been declared dead than film technicians at the 20th Century Fox studios in Johannesburg began work – and worked through the night – on a film, *Dr Verwoerd – A Nation's Tribute*, which, within 24 hours, would start showing at cinemas and drive-ins across the country. All manner of events throughout South Africa were cancelled in deference to a man to whom acres of newsprint were devoted and to whose death the words 'mourning' and 'grief' were unquestioningly attached.

The least sentimental reaction was, predictably, that of the stock market; newspaper readers learned that 'by midday most shares were well on the way to recovering most of their overnight losses,' with gold shares, having opened

17 September Vorster criticises the inclusion of coloured cricketer Basil D'Oliveira in the British MCC team to tour South Africa.
14 November Ciskei 'homeland' is established.

1969

1 February to 21 June Further measures to safeguard 'internal security' introduced.
1 April Public Service Amendment Act establishes the Bureau for State Security (BOSS).

9 April Trial by jury is no more after the Abolition of Juries Act comes into force.
10-16 April Students mount protests to mark the 10th anniversary of the Extension of University Education Act, which enforces the racial segregation of tertiary education.

'sharply lower' the day after Verwoerd's assassination, quickly moving up 'following local and overseas demand'. The fundamentals, not least a political setting of which Verwoerd could claim primary authorship, were unchanged.

This much was obvious when, a little less than a year later, the greater South African leader Albert Luthuli died. Needless to say, there was no urgent film production, or maudlin reportage from the mainstream press. By a kind of visual ventriloquism, the banned – and thus silenced – ANC was eloquent at least in the display of the signature green and black of its flag in the five-hour funeral service at Luthuli's home of Groutville on Natal's North Coast on 21 July 1967. Many mourners wore lapel badges edged with the ANC's colours, and, on its short journey from church to grave, Luthuli's coffin was covered in a green and black pall.

There was no mistaking the regard in which Albert Luthuli was held – not least in the international community. At the graveside, television cameras whirred to the accompaniment of flashbulbs and floodlights, and among the hundreds of mourners were representatives from Britain, the United States, Denmark, Italy, Norway and Sweden. Luthuli was lauded as a 'brave and noble man' by one of the speakers at the funeral who could be quoted, Alan Paton, author of the influential novel *Cry, The Beloved Country*, and national president of the Liberal Party. Like Luthuli, Paton's politics of principle and humanity was thrust aside by apartheid. The non-racial Liberal Party – formed in 1953, though never winning a parliamentary seat – disbanded itself when, in the year after Luthuli's death, the government introduced the Prohibition of Political Interference Act to stop parties from operating across colour lines.

It was clear by then that the death of apartheid's grand theorist would not usher in any softening influences. In a way, it was all too far gone. Early in the year of his assassination, a 'shock' proclamation declared Cape Town's District Six a white group area, which, as one newspaper report put it, 'ripped the heart out of the city's main traditional coloured residential area ... [and] forced the issue of the establishment of a new core of coloured occupation – inevitably on the Cape Flats'.

Every problem foreseen then came about, only in more pronounced and in-tractable form: social dislocation, of which debilitating 21st-century gangsterism

May ANC's Morogoro Conference calls for an intensification of armed and mass political struggles.

13 May Robert Sobukwe is released from Robben Island, but is confined by house arrest to his home in Kimberley.

27 June A Separation of Races law empowers the Secretary for the Interior to change anyone's race classification.

30 June Parliament defines security matters as any matter relating to BOSS and its relationship with any person.

1 July South African Students' Organisation (SASO) launched; Steve Biko elected president.

October *Verkramptes* (hardliners) expelled from the NP; they form the Herstigte Nasionale Party, based on 'exclusive Afrikaner nationalism and true Christian principles'.

and violence remain a lasting consequence; a massive increase in the city's – still unresolved – housing burden; the ever-growing social and economic costs incurred by hugely increasing a commuter population settled far from places of work; and deep mistrust born of what opposition provincial councillor Oscar Wollheim described at the time as the 'cynical dispossession of land owned and occupied over many years by coloured people for the benefit of white people under the cloak of [slum] clearance'.

The destruction of District Six was very much a part of the Verwoerdian grand plan, and there was every sign after his sudden departure that it – and everything else about apartheid – remained central to Nationalist thinking. His successor, John Vorster, oversaw the beginning of massed forced removals that would displace millions of black people to the Bantustans, and presided over new legislation that further criminalised the politics of conscience.

The Terrorism Act of 1967 defined terrorism as anything likely to threaten law and order, granting unlimited powers of arrest, providing for indefinite detention and trials without jury, and transferring the burden of proof to the accused. In equating terrorism with treason, the new law allowed for the execution of apartheid's political opponents. The legislation provoked anxiety even in the pro-government press, with *Die Beeld* newspaper observing that 'the police will now have a free hand to act without legal restraints'.

In the same year, the Defence Amendment Act introduced compulsory military service for all white men, a key measure in the militarisation of the region over the next two decades. Spending on defence soared in this period, rising (in dollar terms) from $63 million in 1960 to $1 billion by the early 1970s (when, under the strictest secrecy, South Africa also began to develop its own nuclear weapons capability, among other things). Added to intensifying international criticism was a new implied threat; following Ian Smith's Unilateral Declaration of Independence in neighbouring Rhodesia in 1965, Nationalist South Africa's sense of the imperative of battle-readiness was stimulated by the emergence of guerrilla opposition close to home.

Yet, at home, Vorster was turning out to be – among whites – the most popular of Nationalist leaders so far, a 1968 survey showing that 82% of white English- and Afrikaans-speaking adults (and 92% of Afrikaners) regarded his leadership

1970

26 February Bantu Homelands Citizenship Act removes South African citizenship from all black people, who are issued with certificates of citizenship for their respective 'homelands'.

14 April UN supports the call to ban South Africa from the Olympic movement.

22 April National Party wins its sixth consecutive election.

April Vorster announces his policy of 'outward movement' - détente.

15 May International Olympic Committee expels South Africa.

19-21 May Vorster visits Malawi.

22 May MCC bows to British government pressure and cancels its intended South African cricket tour.

A bulldozer noses its way into the rubble of yet another demolished block in District Six, Cape Town, a poor, vibrant inner-city precinct destroyed in the name of race-based town planning.

as 'excellent'. In some measure, at least, this was because, unlike his rigidly doctrinaire predecessor, he showed a willingness to be flexible and more open to what in the Nationalist mind might have seemed radical departures – but only in some aspects of public life, and within limits. Verwoerd's unswerving insistence on racial segregation in sport, for instance, was marginally relaxed by Vorster, though his record in this instance – announcing in 1967 that he would not interfere with the selection of players of visiting sports teams, but, just a year later, falling back on habitual obstinacy in the Basil D'Oliveira affair – was less than convincing.

9 June Vorster meets General Franco in Spain.

12 June Installation of Chief Mangosuthu Buthelezi as Chief Executive Officer of the Zululand Territorial Authority.

15 August ANC pamphlet bombs are detonated in several cities.

19 August Chinese people are granted official 'white' status, but only for sport and leisure.

1971

14-21 January Commonwealth meeting in Singapore debates Britain's proposed sale of arms to South Africa.

31 March Bantu Homelands Constitution Act grants increased powers to homeland governments.

28 April Ivory Coast says it is willing to talk to South Africa. Swaziland approves of dialogue, but many other OAU members strongly oppose it.

As their sense of their own successes grew, white South Africans became increasingly touchy about criticism and irritated by what they regarded as misinformed meddling by critics abroad. If, among many of them, just as much irritation was felt about the silliness or unnecessary inconveniences of what was usually lightly referred to as 'petty' apartheid (the grand design being taken more often than not as an accepted condition of regional stability and order), the penalties won against South Africa by activists behind the sports boycott represented a deep thorn in the side of people who wanted to be liked, and who loved their sport.

The intention of England's Marylebone Cricket Club (MCC) to field Basil D'Oliveira, an accomplished all-rounder who had learned his cricket in the streets of the Bo-Kaap in Cape Town, in a visiting team in 1968 proved a snag for Vorster's administration. Foreseeing the risks of political capital being made of D'Oliveira's presence, and the implicit contradiction of allowing him to play, the government refused him entry. The MCC offered a compromise: D'Oliveira would join the tour, but as a correspondent for the *News of the World* newspaper. But the government would not budge. South Africa, Vorster insisted, would not allow sportsmen to be used by 'certain people' as 'pawns in their game to bedevil relations, to create incidents and to undermine our way of life …' The tour was cancelled; 'separate development' trounced fair play.

By the time Dawie de Villiers (later an ambassador, then Nationalist Cabinet minister) led the Springboks on a rugby tour of Britain in 1969, off-the-field protests against 'apartheid sport' were becoming every bit as challenging as the rucks and mauls at the 25-yard line. 'Petty' apartheid was blamed for umpteen missteps in this period, with African-American tennis great Arthur Ashe and a Japanese jockey falling foul of South Africa's inclination to disinvite sportsmen who were not lily-white.

When, in May 1970, Vorster softened again, saying that South Africa was quite happy with an All Blacks touring team that included four 'non-whites' (three Maoris and one Samoan), it was too late. Critics saw through it, perceiving that apartheid South Africa was looking for approval through minor concessions that would leave the core objection unaddressed. This would be the theme of nearly two decades of argument with world opinion.

---

1 May Tswana legislative assembly is established.

6 May Defence minister PW Botha says South Africa is self-sufficient militarily.

1 June Venda and Ciskei territorial authorities are replaced by legislative assemblies.

20 June Organisation of African Unity (OAU) rejects dialogue with South Africa.

21 June International Court of Justice declares that South Africa is obliged to withdraw from Namibia immediately. Vorster says the declaration is not binding.

July SASO adopts its policy manifesto, based on Black Consciousness doctrine.

25 July Joe Kachingwe is appointed Malawi's first ambassador to South Africa.

10 August More ANC pamphlet bombs are set off in four major cities.

A common tendency in South Africa was to view sport as an arena outside politics in which, if only the impediment of racial discrimination were removed, tournaments could go ahead without a fuss. Along these lines, the Springbok cricket captain Ali Bacher declared in 1970, in a cryptic endorsement of greater integration, that 'I believe we must broaden our outlook, to adjust to the era in which we live as far as White and non-White sports is concerned'.

And Vorster seemed to listen. In 1971, the government fashioned a new sports policy, the convolutions of which were matched only by its labyrinthine constitutional 'reforms' a decade hence. The policy laid down that while different races must play their sport separately and in front of segregated audiences, 'multi-racialism' was allowed for sporting events recognised as 'open international', or 'multinational', which meant a 'clearly international event attracting a significant international entry' … except, not surprisingly, in the case of body-contact sports such as boxing, in which case a total ban on mixing remained.

In other areas of life there were similarly bizarre arrangements. At a time when international stars still dared to visit South Africa, the penalties in embarrassment, shame and absurdity were sometimes mind-boggling. When Dame Margot Fonteyn appeared in a performance of *Swan Lake* – for 'non-Whites' only – at the 3 Arts Theatre in Plumstead, Cape Town, in April 1972, *The Argus* newspaper summed up the lunacy:

> *One of the world's greatest artists performed last night – in a theatre that was three-quarters empty. She performed at considerable financial loss to her promoters. Yet thousands upon thousands of people wanted to see her; the whites could not, most non-whites would not, for political reasons. It is an absurd, even fantastic, situation. But it follows logically enough from a political policy solemnly endorsed by most White people in this country. It is a policy not merely tolerated; it is supported with fervour. People go to the voting booths in droves to approve it; intellectuals issue millions of words by hand or mouth in praise of it. Yet it means that an R11-million theatre complex can be built in Cape Town for one race only with the money of all races; and those responsible cheerfully accept any twinges of conscience they might have in a spirit of sacrifice for the national cause. It means that a famous visitor like Dame Margot Fonteyn must dance somewhere else if she wants an audience that includes people other than the ruling whites.*

16-20 August Malawian president Hastings Kamuzu Banda pays a state visit to South Africa.

30 September British and South African navies announce plans for joint manoeuvres in South African waters.

1972

10 February The UN Secretary-General, Dr Kurt Waldheim, announces he has received a formal invitation to visit South Africa for discussions without preconditions. In March, he initiates discussions on Namibia.

April Venda's Legislative Assembly opens.

April to June Widespread student unrest.

24 May Security Intelligence and State Security Council Act esablishes a State Security Council to advise on national policy and strategy on security.

Such 'incidents' were no less than an expression of – and were inseparable from – the larger, expanding architecture of discrimination, which, in the early 1970s, was deepened with the consolidation of the homelands set-up.

Using the Transkei constitution as a template, Vorster's government passed the Bantu Homelands Constitution Act of 1971, which enabled it by proclamation to extend 'self-government' to the myriad bits and pieces of tribal reserves by organising them under Bantustan administrations. In 1972, 19 fragments of land were cobbled together to create a partially self-governing Bophuthatswana. In the same year, Ciskei became partially self-governing. Gazankulu, Venda, QwaQwa and KwaZulu, an amalgam of no fewer than 70 fragments, followed in the next few years.

In most instances, these formed a landscape of infertility or agricultural degradation, with no employment to speak of, and no facilities. Yet the staggering socio-economic deficiencies did nothing to deter the government from clearing so-called 'black spots' in 'white' areas and dumping the people in 'their'

Key figures in the Bantustan schema, tribal chiefs Lucas Mangope of Bophuthatswana (left) and Kaizer Matanzima of Transkei, confer at a homeland leaders' summit in Umtata in 1976.

1 June Bophuthatswana 'homeland' becomes self-governing.

2 June Violent clashes between UCT students and police in Cape Town.

12 June Post Office Amendment Act allows the government to intercept letters and telephone calls. Only Progressive Party MP Helen Suzman votes against it.

1 July Gazankulu 'homeland' holds its first General Assembly.

12 July Black People's Convention is formed, open only to blacks.

1 August Ciskei becomes self-governing.

October A wave of strikes by black workers begins, escalating dramatically in early 1973, chiefly in Durban.

16 December Black People's Convention holds its first national congress.

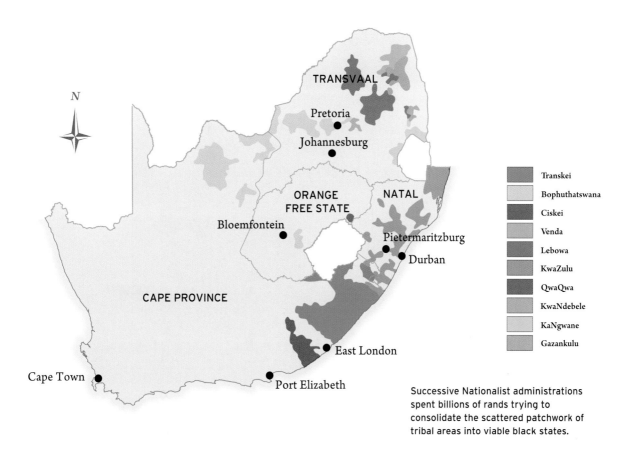

■	Transkei
▫	Bophuthatswana
■	Ciskei
▪	Venda
▪	Lebowa
▪	KwaZulu
■	QwaQwa
▪	KwaNdebele
▪	KaNgwane
▪	Gazankulu

Successive Nationalist administrations spent billions of rands trying to consolidate the scattered patchwork of tribal areas into viable black states.

homelands. Often enough, lorryloads of people were simply abandoned in the bare veld with a water truck and a pile of tents.

* * *

If Vorster was blind to the human and political costs of the Verwoerdian social engineering he showed no reluctance in sustaining, he was freer from the isolationist impulses of his predecessors and seemed to understand better than they did that South Africa belonged in Africa and, even if only from a strategic and economic point of view, had more to gain than lose by trying to win friends elsewhere on the continent. The theory of a measure of regional fraternalism

1973

9 January A Durban strike sparks a wave of labour unrest.

23 January Government announces that the Theron Commission will investigate the political and socio-economic future of coloureds.

1 February Self-government is granted to Venda and Gazankulu.

2 March Restriction orders are issued against six leaders of SASO.

21 March Black Laws Amendment Act is intended to hasten the consolidation of homelands and enable forced removals.

9 April New Zealand says an invitation to an all-white South African rugby team has had to be withdrawn because of its racial selection.

20 April South African police in the Caprivi Strip, Namibia, bordering Zambia, suffer casualties in contacts with 'terrorists'.

Prime Minister John Vorster went out of his way to woo African leaders, Malawi's Hastings Kamuzu Banda being among the few to respond, openly at least.

had, in fact, first been mooted by Verwoerd in 1963, but it was Vorster who gave the so-called 'Outward Policy', or détente, more substance.

In the late 1960s, with world opinion stiffening on apartheid, Vorster sensed that some African leaders at least could be wooed. Within a few years, he had found some common ground with Malawi's Hastings Kamuzu Banda, visited Liberia, met Zambian president Kenneth Kaunda in a railway carriage on the Victoria Falls bridge, and received delegations from the Ivory Coast and Central African Republic.

26 May Sports minister Piet Koornhof announces a new 'multinational sports policy', allowing for mixed sport at international level, and segregated sport at club, provincial and national level.

4 July Bantu Labour Regulations Amendment Act gives blacks the right to strike and gives the Minister of Labour powers to stimulate better working conditions.

5 October Minister of Labour uses his powers under the Bantu Labour Relations Regulation Act to order minimum wage increases of between 50% and 90% for a much of the 100 000 black workforce in the civil engineering sector.

When, in August 1971, Banda visited South Africa, seeing himself as 'a bridge between the races', he told an audience of University of Stellenbosch professors, lecturers and students: 'Do not fall into the trap of your own fear, your own suspicion, distrusting everyone. Just because you have ill will against others, you think they have ill will against you. Don't do that.' A newspaper reported of that gathering that while the 500 professors, lecturers and special student guests in the main hall greeted this cautionary advice in silence, 200 students watching the speech on three closed-circuit television sets in an adjoining hall applauded the Malawian leader. Their applause was almost certainly a meaningful token of the onset of doubt in Afrikanerdom, among the young anyway.

Less than a year later, University of Cape Town students earned struggle cred of their own when baton-wielding police roughly broke up their protest, against discrimination in education, on the steps of St George's Cathedral in the city centre. Much was made of the police ignoring the sanctuary of the church, going as far as grabbing one fleeing protester at the altar and dragging him down the aisle by his hair, beating him continually with their fists.

The resistance of the 1970s, however, would be dominated not by conscientised middle-class white students keen to applaud a rapprochement with Africa or reject racial discrimination in the lecture hall but by a new strand of political thinking among black students that discarded the liberal agenda of white campus politics as much as the Charterist South-Africa-belongs-to-all doctrine of the African National Congress. The man whose name is synonymous with this new black independent-mindedness was Steve Bantu Biko, who, as a Natal University medical student, helped found the South African Students' Organisation (SASO) in 1969.

Biko had been actively engaged in the white-dominated National Union of South African Students (NUSAS) but, with other black students, grew disenchanted with liberal thinking and its insufficiency in expressing black consciousness – ideas and ideals they believed should not rely on any reference to whiteness and the white world of ideas. Furthermore, white student politics had been diluted by the bannings and constant threat of reprisal of the time, and had become more cautious. In contrast, SASO found in the apartheid-created all-black universities of the 1960s what one writer has described as a 'hothouse'

21 October Government bans leaders of SASO, the Black People's Convention, the Black Community Programme, the Black Allied Workers' Union and the Black Workers' Project.

23 November An Arab oil embargo against South Africa, Portugal and Rhodesia, a month after the proclamation of an embargo against the United States and the Netherlands, triggers speculation that petrol rationing is imminent.

1974

30 January United Party-controlled Johannesburg City Council announces the dismantling of petty apartheid measures. Vorster warns that the government will intervene if this campaign causes friction.

for new political thinking. It was here that the Black Consciousness movement, influenced to some extent by the emergence of 'black power' thinking in the United States, took root. The central idea of Black Consciousness, that material liberation must be preceded by a liberation of consciousness, a mental emancipation – 'The most potent weapon in the hands of the aggressor,' Biko once wrote, 'is the mind of the oppressed' – was attractive to young black people. It affirmed them in a society whose political and social arrangements robbed them of self-esteem at every turn.

In 1972, the establishment of the Black People's Convention gave the movement a clearer focus. Even if Black Consciousness was never successful in organising rural or city people in structured opposition or resistance, its ideas were deeply influential among students and young urban blacks wholly unconvinced by liberal opposition, and disappointed by the lack of action on the part of the banned liberation movements.

The government perceived the risk of a new front of resistance developing in the name of Black Consciousness and, in 1973, imposed banning orders and restrictions on its leaders. The organisations themselves would be banned later, too. The Vorster administration's characteristically heavy-handed response prompted Helen Suzman to warn that 'the younger generation of blacks are simply not prepared to take suppressive policies lying down any longer.' The government could ban leaders, and others would rise up in their place because apartheid had 'spawned an indestructible black nationalism which all of us are going to live to regret and which is, after all, only a by-product of white nationalism'. Not for the first time, or the last, Suzman was spot-on, though hers was an opinion lightly discounted.

* * *

By the early 1970s, the good times of the 1960s were over – and partly because of that decade's economic successes. Demand for skilled labour, in the growing manufacturing sector especially, had sponsored a wholesale evasion of laws intended to limit the scale of black employment in the cities, heightening black aspirations and giving labour greater purchase both economically and politically. In the first two years of the 1970s, the gap between white and black wages began

March Riotous Assemblies Amendment Act allows the government to ban any gathering of more than one person, legal or not, if it threatens law and order. A second law, the Affected Organisations Act, seeks to stop foreign funding for political activities.

20 March Vorster reacts to Britain's reimposition of the ban on arms sales, saying South Africa does not need them.
April Paraguayan dictator Alfredo Stroessner visits South Africa.

24 April National Party wins its seventh general election; the Progressive Party grows from one to six MPs.
25 April World Council of Churches calls on banks to disinvest from South Africa.

to narrow for the first time, but the trend was stayed by a recession that followed a drop in the gold price and rising inflation, chiefly as a result of the 1973 oil price hike by the Organisation of Petroleum Exporting Countries (OPEC).

The downturn triggered a round of strikes in Natal, the eastern Cape and the Rand, which signalled the end of the old way of conducting labour relations with black workers. Black unions were not illegal, but black workers were excluded from collective bargaining mechanisms. From the early 1970s, corporate managements began to see the wisdom and the necessity of establishing formal labour relations with a workforce whose cooperation they counted on, a change of heart which impelled the government to begin to confront the reality that economic growth depended on more stable black communities in urban areas. This meant an inevitable dilution of apartheid doctrine.

Such shifts, along with the slight and convoluted 'reforms' in sports policy and Vorster's African détente initiatives, widened fissures in Nationalist ranks between *verligte* (enlightened) and *verkrampte* (hardline) thinking. The 1969 expulsion of hardliners, who formed the Herstigte Nasionale Party (HNP), did not immediately register in electoral terms, but the 1974 general election illustrated changes in white political sentiment that would become increasingly pronounced. After her 13 solo years, Helen Suzman was joined by six new Progressive Party MPs. The United Party was still the official opposition, though its share of votes continued to decline. To the right of the Nationalists, the HNP fielded 48 candidates, garnering some 39 500 votes, though failing to win a single seat. To the right even of the HNP, Eugène Terre'Blanche's ultra-right-wing Afrikaner Weerstandsbeweging (AWB) was formed in this period, too, at a meeting in a garage in the Transvaal town of Heidelberg in 1973.

Black Consciousness icon Steve Bantu Biko is memorialised on the cover of *Drum* magazine after his death in detention in September 1977.

---

6 **May** British Lions rugby team begins a controversial 22-match tour of South Africa and Rhodesia.

15 **June** Defence minister PW Botha says on a visit to the Caprivi Strip that the SADF has taken over from police as the defenders of the country's northern borders.

7 **July** New Zealand imposes a blanket ban on virtually all visits by South African sports teams.

23 **July** In the wake of Nationalist criticism, newspapers adopt a code of conduct under the National Press Union. It is strongly criticised by editors and academics.

26 **August** Defence Act amendment creates penalties for resisting military service.

16 **September** US agrees to sell helicopters and reconnaissance aircraft to South Africa.

21 **September** Vorster pays secret visit to Ivory Coast for talks with President Félix Houphouët-Boigny.

Yet, after what might be characterised as the delusion of supremacy of the 1960s, the scope for white political action which ignored the fundamentals of the South African reality – the interdependence of white interests and black aspirations – was narrowing. This was compounded by black assertiveness beyond the country's immediate borders when, following the 1974 revolution in Portugal, the old, and costly, Portuguese colonies of Angola and Mozambique were cut loose.

*   *   *

Vorster's keenness to work with Zambian president Kenneth Kaunda in trying to convince a recalcitrant Ian Smith to negotiate with his overwhelming opposition in Rhodesia reflected a grasp of southern African realities that would be sorely tested once Portugal ceded independence to Mozambique and Angola in June and November 1975. Both states had been embroiled in anti-colonial guerrilla conflict for a long time, but, with independence, the freedom fighters of the MPLA in Angola and FRELIMO in Mozambique became the rulers, adding pressing complexity to Vorster's African diplomacy.

He moved to build friendly relations – and seal them with economic co-operation – with Samora Machel's government in Maputo, winning, for the time being, an undertaking that Mozambique would not allow itself to be used as a forward base for guerrilla activity by South Africa's liberation movements.

The Angolan question was more complex. Angolans' own loyalties were divided between at least three liberation movements, and, though the Marxist-aligned MPLA was the dominant one, some African leaders (such as Kaunda) and the Western powers, France and the United States in particular, quietly encouraged Vorster to wade in on the side of the MPLA's opponents in the pro-West UNITA movement and the third group, the FNLA, in the months before independence.

As Portuguese colonial refugees fled the embattled region – many abandoning their vehicles on the northern bank of the Kunene River and swimming across, some managing to float cars across on rafts – South Africa was mustering a force to go the other way. Oil-rich Angola was no doubt perceived in Cold War terms as a strategic asset best kept in the Western fold; both France and the United States offered weapons to Pretoria as an inducement. However, the launching of Operation

---

25 September SASO and the Black People's Convention hold 'Viva FRELIMO' rallies to celebrate the end of Portuguese rule in Mozambique. Terrorism Act charges are brought against organisers and participants.

14 October Sports minister Piet Koornhof announces a relaxation of apartheid rules for sport.
1 November QwaQwa becomes self-governing.

1975

11 February Vorster visits Liberia for talks with President William Tolbert.
26 February South Africa signs a trade agreement with Taiwan.

Savannah in the second half of 1975 was ill-judged; having got to within 12km of Luanda, the South African armoured column was forced to withdraw after FNLA troops failed to wrest control of Luanda from the MPLA. Even as Zambia and Zaire willed Vorster to maintain pressure on the MPLA, which was supported by a contingent of Soviet-armed Cuban troops and Soviet military advisers, the South African leader was doubtful about the risks. These were confirmed when the US Senate, objecting to not having been consulted, blocked further assistance to anti-MPLA forces. Vorster decided to pull out.

At home, there was joy and celebration among families and sweethearts of returning soldiers – troop trains, daubed with slogans, fluttered with toilet-paper streamers as they pulled into clamorous stations – but in the greater scheme there was little to celebrate. Within a month of South Africa's withdrawal from Angola in early 1976, the Organisation of African Unity (OAU) recognised the MPLA

South Africa's foray into Angola in 1975 – encouraged by anti-Soviet Western and African governments – ended in withdrawal and embarrassment, but stimulated Pretoria's lasting military involvement in the region.

10 March South African police in Rhodesia are confined to camps as South Africa begins disengaging from the Rhodesian process. The final withdrawal of police is ordered on 1 August.

17 and 18 March Vorster and Rhodesian premier Ian Smith meet in Cape Town to discuss Rhodesia's future.
26 March Finance minister Owen Horwood announces a 36% rise in proposed defence expenditure.

27 March Plans announced to reduce homeland areas from 113 to 36.
12 April Atlas Aircraft Corporation delivers the first series of Impala Mk II jet fighters.
24 April Defence Act amendment gives black and white military officers equal status.

government in Luanda. The whole exercise, as the Reader's Digest *Illustrated History of South Africa* describes it, 'had cost Pretoria dearly: the détente policy with Africa was up in smoke, the military had lost face, there was a large communist presence on the doorstep and France had been lost as a supplier of weapons.' Furthermore, Angola was understandably hostile, and more than willing to allow its territory to be used as a springboard for attacks to the south by guerrillas of the South West African People's Organisation (SWAPO). South Africa felt compelled to dig in across the northern sector of South West Africa – the 'Border' or 'operational area' with which thousands of conscripted white soldiers would become grimly familiar over the next decade – to try to stem armed incursions and keep a war of liberation at least one state away. On a scale larger than ever before, the military became a central factor in southern African politics, and in the defence of apartheid.

All the while, South Africa continued to grapple with the challenges of making its grand plan hold up. The National Party remained as resistant as ever to reformist thinking, dismissing out of hand, for instance, the mid-1976 Theron Commission recommendation that coloured people be given direct representation in government. The commission, headed by Stellenbosch academic Erika Theron, broke new ground by including members who were not white. If its ideas began slowly to percolate through Nationalist thinking, not even its recommendations to repeal the Mixed Marriages Act and the sex-across-the-colour-bar clause in the Immorality Act were accepted. Later in the year, the Transkei was granted 'independence', a peremptory event of which one newspaper said that as the new state 'celebrates its arrival on the map of southern Africa, the half-finished projects about the streets of its capital, Umtata, scaffolding and wet cement, symbolize the haste and uncertain hopes with which the new country has been thrust to birth'. But all these things, the *faux* statecraft and the institutional tinkering, were dwarfed in significance by the popular revolt of schoolchildren in the Soweto uprising of 16 June.

The protest caught the government off balance, triggering a national surge of resistance, and took the liberation movements completely by surprise, too. But it was, in fact, wholly predictable, the result of a crisis that, even as it grew during May and the first two weeks of June, was recklessly ignored.

---

1 May Home ownership and trading rights are accorded to urban blacks.
6 May Government says its aim is to give all black children free and compulsory education as soon as possible.
8 May Bram Fischer dies in prison.

25 June Mozambique becomes independent under FRELIMO.
23 July South African Council of Churches warns that unless racial policies are reversed there will be no peace.

12 August A statement issued in Lusaka and Salisbury gives details of proposals agreed to in talks between Vorster and Smith, which could lead to a settlement in Rhodesia.
25 August Vorster and Zambian president Kenneth Kaunda meet at Victoria Falls.

Anger among black schoolchildren had been mounting for months following the pig-headedly irrational decree of late 1974 by Transvaal education authorities that Afrikaans be used equally with English as the medium of tuition in black schools. This was, as historian David Welsh has pointed out, a striking instance of the impact on racial policy of the lingering pettiness of ethnic animosity between Afrikaner and English South Africans; the Nationalists resented the preponderance of English and the production of 'black Englishmen', as Verwoerd had cast it – just as, no doubt, Afrikaans publishers resented the lost opportunities in a lucrative textbook market.

The man who drove the policy was the *verkrampte* Nationalist Andries Treurnicht, the Deputy Minister of Bantu Education (later the leader of the breakaway Conservative Party) who turned a blind eye to the mounting crisis. One who was especially conscious of the 'very serious' tension in Soweto in the weeks before the uprising was Fred van Wyk, director of the South African Institute of Race Relations, who raised his anxieties with Progressive Reform Party MP René de Villiers in the hope that, if the government could be convinced of the risks, sense would prevail. In early May, however, Treurnicht's indifference was evident when he responded, 'I am not aware of any real problem.' When, in the last week of May, class boycotts had spread to six schools, the department threatened simply to shut them down and expel protesters. Van Wyk tried again, sending a second warning by telegram on 11 June, but again without success.

For some, the delusion of black acquiescence still ran deep. In a parliamentary debate on 15 June, the Nationalist MP for Ermelo, GF Botha, berated liberal politicians, saying 'the fear and pessimism shown by the Opposition can do a great deal of harm to the economy'. Not everyone was blinkered. In the same debate, Alex Boraine, then a Progressive Reform Party MP – he later turned his back on the 'pointlessness' of parliamentary politics, playing a key role in the 1980s in forging opportunities for white and black nationalists to meet and imagine a shared future – cautioned MPs against mistaking their destiny: 'We have built this country together, not separately,' he said, 'and ... the future will depend on our ability to work in partnership.'

Just one day later, early on the cold, sunny Transvaal winter morning of Wednesday 16 June, Soweto's children set off for school without betraying to

30 September Winnie Mandela is released from her banning order and house arrest; on 5 October she ends 13 years of forced silence with a strong attack on the country's Terrorism Act.

26 November Afrikaans writer Breyten Breytenbach is sentenced in Pretoria to nine years' imprisonment for Terrorism Act offences. He has pleaded guilty to entering South Africa to start an organisation, Atlas or Okhela, intended to be the white wing of the ANC.

1976

1 January Centre Against Apartheid established at the UN.
5 January Television launched in South Africa.

parents or anyone else – especially the many *impimpi* (police informers) – the well-kept secret of their plan to take a massed stand against being made to learn their lessons in what was widely regarded as the 'language of the oppressor'. An hour before the planned 7am start of the protest, hundreds of pupils began assembling at prearranged points, some carrying hastily scrawled placards with slogans such as 'To Hell with Bantu Education' and 'Down with Afrikaans'. No sooner had the marchers set out for Orlando Stadium than the police moved to block them. The standoff came to a head shortly after 9am when police hurled a tear gas canister into the crowd hoping to scatter the protesters. Seconds later, a single shot was fired. Panic ensued. Some threw stones, and the police fired again, repeatedly. In those few seconds of violence, the country was jerked into crisis.

The defining moment of the tragedy was captured in Sam Nzima's photograph of the bloodied body of 13-year-old Hector Petersen, borne at a run, a dead weight in the arms of a fellow student. The image sooned gained emblematic status as a symbol of state violence and black rage.

An unnamed reporter from the *Star* newspaper in Johannesburg described his experience of 16 June as 'the most terrifying day of my life as I lay caught between the crossfire of police bullets and stones from enraged students on the rampage'. In living rooms across the country, the vicarious experience was no less impressive – frightening for most whites, encouraging for many blacks – for television was just six months old in South Africa, and the nightly coverage of the spreading violence, the defiant crowds and smoky mayhem registered as an inescapable challenge to many certainties.

The government saw its task as restoring order 'to free South Africa from thugs in the streets of Soweto and elsewhere', as Justice minister Jimmy Kruger told Parliament in a snap debate a day later, on 17 June.

Bitterness would soon displace the smiles of these Soweto pupils demonstrating against enforced Afrikaans tuition on 16 June 1976 when police opened fire on the protest. Weeks of violence followed, spreading throughout the country.

January to May Protests at Soweto schools over forced Afrikaans tuition escalate.

22 January Dr Andries Treurnicht, the former chairman of the Afrikaner Broederbond, is appointed Deputy Minister of Bantu Administration and Bantu Education.

5 February Defence Amendment Act allows conscripted troops to serve anywhere outside South Africa.

7 February Apartheid laws are suspended at 16 hotels, allowing them to cater for all races.

4 March Vorster warns of the 'aggravating factor' of Russian and Cuban involvement in southern Africa.

12 March It is announced that virtually all South African troops have been withdrawn from Angola.

---

14 March Chief Mangosuthu Buthelezi denounces the homelands policy, saying the country must move towards majority rule.

20 March Roman Catholic Church decides in principle to open its 192 all-white schools to black pupils.

29 May Eskom announces it has decided to order two nuclear power plants from France.

11 June Treurnicht rejects applications by five Soweto schools to depart from the so-called 50-50 (equal use of English and Afrikaans) policy.

16 June Soweto uprising begins, spreading across the Rand and to other parts of the country in the days and weeks to come.

18 June Theron Commission recommends the restoration of political rights to coloureds, which the government later rejects.

FORTRESS APARTHEID – 1965-76   **107**

6 July Government scraps compulsory teaching in Afrikaans in black schools.

29 August Vorster, on his tenth anniversary as prime minister, acknowledes that the country has problems, but rejects the idea that they constitute a crisis.

3-6 September Vorster and US Secretary of State Henry Kissinger meet in Zurich to discuss negotiations on independence in Namibia and majority rule in Rhodesia.

29 September Jeremy Cronin is sentenced to ten years' imprisonment for offences under the Terrorism and Internal Security Acts, to which he pleads guilty.

26 October South Africa proclaims the 'independence' of Transkei. The UN immediately rejects it as invalid.

Police showed no hesitation in using their considerable powers of detention to try to neutralise the new threat.

Although it initially dismissed the 'alleged aversion to Afrikaans' as the prime reason for the 'demonstrations', the government backed down on the inflammatory directive on Afrikaans tuition. But the crisis was far wider. Violence and deaths, protests and stayaways spread over the next year as the idea, and the power, of mass action was renewed across the country; international pressure intensified, and thousands of young black people slipped across the borders to join the liberation movements and continue the fight. The ANC in particular grasped the opportunity to reassert itself. The atmosphere at home produced a new generation of supporters, including growing numbers of young white people. Umkhonto we Sizwe had not fired a shot in South Africa in almost a decade and a half since its founding in 1961, but, within a year of Soweto, the first insurgents of the class of 1976 were infiltrating the apartheid state bearing AK-47s, hand grenades and limpet mines.

As Sharpeville redefined the political contest of the 1960s, turning protest against discrimination into an armed struggle for national liberation from minority rule, so did the Soweto uprising a decade and half later reinvigorate the struggle, as well as ushering in a phase of low-level civil war in which townships eventually became battle zones, patrolled by armed troops and revolutionary-minded 'comrades'. 'Apartheid was beginning to fail,' historian Nigel Worden writes of this period, 'although this was not fully apparent until the 1980s, and it was still to take an unconscionable time to die.' Soon, the terminology of 'fortress apartheid' – a 'total strategy' to meet a 'total onslaught' – would express the beleaguered state of white nationalism. Soweto started the South African revolution, though, arguably, it was a revolution that would not run its course; a costly and ultimately inconclusive cycle of repression and revolt was about to begin.

The Soweto uprising of 1976 triggered mass protests across the country and reinvigorated the struggle against oppression.

---

11 November UN adopts nine resolutions against apartheid at the end of a two-and-a-half week debate on the South African question.

24 November An estimated 700 school pupils and students from Soweto who fled to Botswana, Swaziland and Lesotho after 16 June reject the government's amnesty offer, which expired on 22 November.

December Leaders of the September 1974 'Viva FRELIMO' rallies are sentenced to terms on Robben Island.

CHAPTER FOUR

The stalemate years

1977-85

Mourners make way for the coffin of one of the Cradock Four – activists Matthew Goniwe, Fort Calata, Sparrow Mkonto and Sicelo Mhlauli – murdered by security police in June 1985. The mass funeral was the catalyst for a partial state of emergency in the eastern Cape.

After Soweto, black political thinking and action became, for the first time since 1948, the inescapably central factor of the South African future. Arguably, this had always been so, but from the late 1970s, the hard facts could no longer be wished away. Repression would intensify, and there would be reforms tailored to preserve minority rule by appeasing blacks through a marginal easing of political and socio-economic discrimination, but the majority's fundamental demands would remain unalterably compelling. Equally, while the African National Congress, as the biggest and best organised of the liberation movements, acted swiftly and successfully to capitalise on post-Soweto fervour, the custodians of the struggle would have to confront in the next decade the prospect of either a costly stalemate or a rapprochement that would call for deft political arts, and compromise.

The white community was politically and morally challenged as never before. The immediacy of television footage from beyond the railway tracks disabused the beneficiaries of apartheid of their notion that blacks were happier and better off for the beer halls and bus services delivered by a white-led state and economy. International criticism grew by the year.

Even bedside reading for the steadily expanding Afrikaner middle class, as much as for English-speakers, became increasingly unsettling. Alongside such literary explorations of the local trauma as JM Coetzee's *In the Heart of the Country* (1977) and Nadine Gordimer's *The Conservationist* (1974), a wider readership confronted their own troubling tales in popular fiction such as Elsa Joubert's *The Long Journey of Poppie Nongena* (1978) and the novels of André Brink, including *A Dry White Season* (1979; banned at the time for its negative portrayal of the security police) and *Rumours of Rain* (1978). Black writing by, among others, playwright Zakes Mda and poets Mongane Wally Serote and Sipho Sepamla, began to gain a wider, and white, audience.

Anxieties in the boardroom – partly about rising radical socialism undermining the prospects of profit-driven market economics – prompted business

1977

25 January Indemnity Bill, retroactive to 16 June 1976, gives security forces immunity from prosecution if acting in good faith to prevent disorder.

1 February KwaZulu proclaimed a self-governing territory.

1 April Roelof 'Pik' Botha becomes Minister of Foreign Affairs.

25 April Journalists are allowed to visit Robben Island for the first time.

May Defence Act amendment doubles period of conscription from one to two years.

16 May Winnie Mandela, restricted to Soweto since on 28 December 1976, is banished to Brandfort township in the Orange Free State.

leaders, including English and Afrikaner corporate titans Harry Oppenheimer of Anglo American and Anton Rupert of the Rembrandt Group, to forge a proactive agenda. The result in March 1977 was the Urban Foundation, an initiative to boost black opportunities in education, homeownership and business, and to lobby the government to face up to the importance of permanent, stable black communities in the cities.

John Vorster's last months in politics, as State President – here, addressing Parliament in February 1979 – were overshadowed by the Information Scandal.

Political shifts among whites showed in the 1977 general election when, after the disintegration of the old United Party, the Progressive Federal Party (renamed from the Progressive Reform Party) became the official opposition. Their tally of only 17 seats (and 17% of the vote) was dwarfed by the National Party's landslide performance (65% of the vote, earning them 134 seats), but it

19 & 20 May US Vice President Walter Mondale and Vorster meet in Vienna for talks.

21 & 22 May US Ambassador to the United Nations, Andrew Young, visits South Africa at the invitation of Harry Oppenheimer,

and meets black and white community leaders and others. He argues that economic pressure can bring change.

11 June University of Stellenbosch announces that postgraduate degree courses will be open to black, coloured and Indian students,

along with undergraduate courses not offered at 'their own' universities.

28 June United Party is dissolved. Sir De Villiers Graaff announces his retirement from politics on 5 October, having been leader of the opposition from 1956.

generated parliamentary debate more hostile to the apartheid project than at any time since 1948. In the same year – as the burgeoning security establishment snared thousands of detainees – white conscription was doubled from one to two years.

A little more than a year after John Vorster was persuading his followers that South Africa, unlike the rest of the West, was 'not scared to step forward and take up the fight for democracy' – he was still smarting at having had the rug of United States support pulled from under him during the Angolan debacle – the apartheid state was chiefly engaged in doing battle on its own beleaguered behalf. In its desperation, white political authority became prone to increasing depravity, grimly illustrated in the death of a detainee in the second week of September 1977.

Deaths in detention were not new. Between 1960 and the mid-1970s, 45 detainees had died in police hands – usually, police said baldly, by committing suicide by hanging themselves in their cells, or as a result of slipping in the shower and banging their heads, or by leaping out of or falling from the windows of multi-storey police buildings. Interrogation, it seems, was always conducted on the upper floors.

But the 46th death was different, not only in that the man himself, Steve Bantu Biko, was an influential leader, but in that the way he died so pitiably exposed the poverty of morality at the heart of the state. Biko, who had eluded police for a year, was on his way to Cape Town in mid-August – to distribute pamphlets 'inciting blacks to cause riots', police said – when he was arrested at a roadblock outside Grahamstown and taken in under section 6 of the Terrorism Act, which allowed for indefinite detention. He was driven the next day to Port Elizabeth where he was stripped naked and held in various cells for the next two weeks. Still naked, but placed in leg irons, he was taken to police headquarters on 6 September where he was interrogated by five security police officers.

On that day, or soon after, he was rammed against a wall so hard that he sustained the brain injury that would kill him. (Police said at the inquest that

Steve Biko's coffin, borne on an ox-cart, is accompanied by thousands of mourners who poured into King William's Town from around the country for the Black Consciousness leader's September 1977 funeral.

July Criminal Procedure Act dispenses with 'innocent until proven guilty' precept.

August & September Government's constitutional proposals are rejected by black and coloured leaders and criticised by white opposition leaders and academics.

10 August About 100 white sympathisers join evicted black squatters in a passive protest against the demolition of shanty dwellings outside Cape Town. This is the third day of an operation to remove an estimated 26 000 squatters from three camps.

12 September Steve Biko dies in detention; 15 000 attend his funeral in King William's Town on 25 September. A 15-day inquest ends on 2 December with a finding that no one can be held criminally responsible for his death.

19 **October** Government bans all 17 movements affiliated with the Black Consciousness Movement, including the Black People's Convention, SASO and Black Women's Federation, and closes the *World* and *Weekend World* newspapers.

3 **November** Vorster announces that influx control regulations are to be amended to provide greater freedom of movement for urban blacks. 'Pass books' are to be abolished and replaced by documents issued by the 'homeland' governments.

10 **November** Finance minister Owen Horwood announces a R250 million low-cost housing programme for blacks, coloureds and Indians, and security of tenure for blacks in urban areas.

he banged his head in a scuffle, though admitted what had really happened to the Truth and Reconciliation Commission in the late 1990s.) Biko didn't die immediately, but it was clear to his persecutors that something was very wrong. They called in no fewer than three state doctors who made false diagnoses to protect the interrogators.

When Biko's condition became grave, and police were urged to take him to hospital, he was dumped, naked and unconscious, in the back of a police van and driven 1 600km to Pretoria. There, on 12 September, he 'died a miserable and lonely death on a mat on the stone floor of a prison cell', as the Biko family's lawyer Sydney Kentridge described it at the inquest into the Black Consciousness leader's death, in early December. The three-week proceeding concluded with magistrate MJ Prins's finding that no one could be held criminally responsible for Steve Biko's death.

The government's reaction – and probably the reaction of most whites, too – to the deaths of people held as a threat to order, or the status quo, was invariably one of indifference. But the announcement of Steve Biko's death is remembered for the particularly callous reaction of Minister of Police Jimmy Kruger, and of his audience, the delegates to the National Party's Transvaal congress. Newspaper reports described 'ripples of laughter' from the party faithful as Kruger explained the circumstances of Biko's arrest and interrogation. Of his death, Kruger said finally: 'I am not glad and I am not sorry about Mr Biko. It leaves me cold. I can say nothing to you.' Not content with that, he went on, if somewhat haltingly, in mockingly comic fashion – rewarded with more laughter – 'Any person who dies … I shall also be sorry if I die.'

A day later, on 15 September, newspaper reports described how between 1 200 and 1 300 University of Fort Hare students, who had gathered to honour Biko, were arrested and detained for holding a mass open-air meeting in contravention of the Prohibition of Gatherings Act. An exercise of such extravagant law-keeping could only have signalled the faltering authority of the state, a quality underscored by the emphatic detail in one report that 'the students almost willingly climbed into police vehicles, many giving the Black Power salute'. Upwards of 18 000 mourners gathered in cold, rainy weather at the Victoria sports ground in King William's Town to bury Biko on 16 September. The crowd would

---

13 November Bishop Desmond Tutu becomes secretary-general of the South African Council of Churches.

24 November A bomb explodes in the Carlton Centre in Johannesburg, injuring 16 people.

30 November National Party wins landslide victory in general election. Progressive Federal Party (PFP) becomes official opposition, with 17 seats.

6 December Bophuthatswana 'homeland' becomes 'independent'. Chief Lucas Mangope is elected president.

20 December Canada announces withdrawal of government support for trade with South Africa.

have been larger by many thousands more had the authorities not turned them back at roadblocks on routes leading to King William's Town. Within the month, Black Consciousness organisations and their leaders were banned, the *World* newspaper (which was hospitable to Black Consciousness thinking) was shut down, and its editor Percy Qoboza detained – and yet pressure on the Nationalists only mounted.

The United Nations Security Council imposed a mandatory arms embargo just as the establishment of guerrilla bases and liberation movement cells in the so-called frontline states of southern Africa extended the scope of insurgency and heightened the prospect of escalating military conflict. In the event, sanctions of this kind seemed only – in the short term anyway – to stimulate the homegrown defence industry and, no doubt, the bloody-minded bellicosity of the Vorster government. In not so many years, South African fighter jets, special forces and the murky figures of a growing clandestine counterinsurgency complex would strike across the borders of neighbouring countries with missiles and letter bombs.

While bannings and mass detentions hampered activism at home, under Oliver Tambo's leadership the ANC not only survived the dislocation imposed by exile, but succeeded in projecting itself as the primary vehicle of liberation. It became the focus of growing international solidarity, and maintained its visibility as a beacon for resistance at home. The revival of the struggle under the influence, if not the banner, of the Black Consciousness Movement enabled the ANC to galvanise its own ranks and win over Africanists among the thousands of young disaffected black people who were impatient to play a more active role.

This impatience is reflected in the testimony in 1978 of a young guerrilla – one of those who left the country after Soweto – who was arrested on his return on an armed mission. The young accused – Mosima Gabriel 'Tokyo' Sexwale, who rose to become a key ANC leader, Premier of Gauteng province after 1994 and, later, a leading light in the multi-billion-rand mining sector of the post-apartheid economy – told the Pretoria Supreme Court of his dawning political consciousness in the early 1970s. By the time he went to Soweto's Orlando West High School, he said, he was 'already beginning to question the injustice of the society … and to ask why nothing was being done to change it'.

1978

6 January Donald Woods, banned editor of the *Daily Dispatch*, goes into exile.

8 January Political scientist and author Richard Turner, banned in 1973, is assassinated in Durban by an untraced killer.

27 February Robert Sobukwe, founder of the PAC, dies at 53, and is buried at his home town, Graaff-Reinet.

April Police confirm ANC guerrillas have been involved in skirmishes with counter-insurgency forces in the Eastern Transvaal.

April Azanian People's Organisation (AZAPO) is formed at an inaugural conference at Roodepoort. It is open to blacks, coloureds and Indians, but not whites, and opposes all institutions created by the government.

Their downcast looks speak volumes as Prime Minister John Vorster and his Information minister, Connie Mulder, address a press conference on the damning Information Scandal, for which both lost their jobs.

Within the inner circles of white nationalism, 'change' was being talked about all the more feverishly, too, but in the febrile conditions of secrecy, paranoia and desperation, the initial results were disastrous. Convincing themselves that winning friends – along the lines of the African détente initiatives – was the way to go, expensive and far-fetched plans by the Department of Information won approval from Vorster and other senior government men. As a result, millions of rands, chiefly from secret Defence funds, were squandered on covert projects through which South Africa hoped to engineer good public relations.

The government often genuinely felt that, in the idiom of the time, it was 'moving in the right direction', if only the world would acknowledge it and their black opponents abandon such radical demands as one man, one vote. In the very month of Biko's death, for instance, much was made of the scrapping of 'police station apartheid', as one headline described it, the report informing readers: 'Apartheid has been outlawed at police charge offices throughout the country – segregation signs are to come down, while black officers may now wear the same uniform as whites.' With clearly unintended irony, a police spokesman said approvingly, 'They already wear the same riot uniforms, so this is just an extension.'

But the multi-million-rand spin project masterminded by the Department of Information took the hard sell to new levels. The most egregious enterprise, coyly named Project Annemarie, gave the National Party a warmly disposed English-language newspaper, *The Citizen*, at a cost to taxpayers of R31.9 million. In all, Defence and Bureau for State Security allocations totalling R64 million were splurged in South Africa and abroad on this and other ill-conceived efforts to

4 May South African troops attack Cassinga in Angola, killing hundreds of SWAPO refugees.
8 May Vorster says he personally authorised the Department of Information to use secret funds without parliamentary approval for purposes 'in the highest national interest'.

24 May Laws to address black grievances provide for 99-year leases in townships, new 'travel documents', and replacing the word 'Bantu' with 'black' in all legislation.
June Department of Information is disbanded.

September Vorster resigns (and is elected State President), and PW Botha becomes NP leader and Prime Minister.
2 November Justice Anton Mostert's commission of inquiry into the Information Scandal uncovers corruption and fraud.

secretly bolster the country's standing. Mounting disquiet in Nationalist ranks, along with embarrassing investigative journalism that blew the government's cover, compelled Vorster to resign as Prime Minister, and assume for a while the titular position of State President. The subsequent judicial inquiry under Judge Rudolph Erasmus confirmed Vorster's disgrace – he left public life altogether – and that of Information minister Connie Mulder, the NP's Transvaal leader.

The Information Scandal – or Muldergate – stimulated a certain democratic resolve in the rotten state, and, in a curious way, provided an anxious white public with a distracting sideshow. The Erasmus Commission's final report, one journalist wrote, was like an action-packed novel, the last dramatic chapter of disclosures telling of 'flashy cars, expensive holidays, jet-setting, and deals in which millions of rands changed hands secretly'. But the real challenges were entirely unaffected by the spectacle.

Some months before the final word was spoken on the Info saga, an *Argus* editorial of July 1978 described the climacteric: 'Thinking Nationalists and their political opponents are saying much the same thing … there is growing consensus that radical and dramatic action must be taken now to stop the drift to disaster. And there is only one way to move … It is towards dialogue and negotiation, towards the full participation of all races, towards sharing – either of power or of land. Nothing less will save us.'

The fall of John Vorster, and the scotching of Transvaal leader Mulder's hopes of succeeding him as Prime Minister, opened the way to Defence minister PW Botha. He was the first leader who was not either a lawyer, cleric or academic, having made a life of serving the NP from the mid-1930s when he dropped out of university. Narrow party ambitions, critics said, drove this dour, hawkish career politician. Yet, for all his shortcomings, he was an important agent of reforms which, either because of what they achieved, or what they failed to achieve, nudged South Africa towards settling the central issue of citizenship.

There is a double irony in the fact that PW Botha was the man who made the notion of 'change' acceptable. On the one hand, where changes he presided over 'went too far', they succeeded chiefly in splitting the National Party. On the other, where they failed to go far enough, they exposed the government to a political crisis it could not survive.

---

7 December Vorster opens the first emergency session of Parliament to be held in peacetime, promising action against anyone guilty of maladministration in the Information Scandal.

1979

ANC declares 1979 the Year of the Spear.
13 January Clash between police and suspected guerrillas is reported near the Botswana border.

2 February Vorster promises a new deal – new economic and financial measures and a new constitutional dispensation.
6 April Dr Connie Mulder is expelled from the National Party over his role in the Information Scandal.

He made a promising start, telling the country – it was a message mainly for white voters – that change was unavoidable. 'We are moving in a changing world,' Botha said in one of his first speeches as Prime Minister.

We must adapt otherwise we shall die … The moment you start oppressing people … they fight back … We must acknowledge people's rights and … make ourselves free by giving to others in a spirit of justice what we demand for ourselves … A white monopoly of power is untenable in the Africa of today … A meaningful division of power is needed between all race groups … Apartheid is a recipe for permanent conflict.

His stark metaphor, 'adapt or die' – satirised at the time as 'adapt or dye' – alarmed conservatives, and for good reason, since, as the writer André Brink noted just a few years later in 1981, Botha had 'introduced the possibility of change and that may carry him or other people further'. Brink professed himself 'totally cynical' about Botha, but observed: 'Once a certain historical momentum is created I don't think it can be stopped.'

The problem was that, rather like their predecessors in DF Malan's government of 1948, Botha's Nationalists had no clear idea of what to make of their historical moment, except to fall back on instinctive self-interest. In the late 1940s, the Nationalists sought to shore up their power in order to implement apartheid; in the late 1970s, their successors were intent on reinforcing their power in order to attempt the system's limited and piecemeal modification. The glaring flaw was that the only credible reform option lay in a meaningful ceding of power.

The idea of 'separate development' was every day undermined by a socio-economic environment in which the needs of black workers and their families, and equally of shareholders and factory managers, could only be met by defying the complex of apartheid laws enacted to segregate society and economy by race. The pace of urbanisation, for which cities were ill-prepared, produced vast 'squatter camps' of 'illegal immigrants' from the Bantustans. The western Cape, defined by the Nationalists as a so-called 'coloured labour preference area' from which black people were excluded by influx control, began to absorb many thousands of desperate job-seekers from the Ciskei and Transkei. By law, towns and cities could be regarded as home only by black people with 'section 10' rights (for those born there, or who had worked for one employer for ten years, or were

---

1 May First Wiehahn Commission report recommends registration of black trade unions, abolition of the principle of statutory job reservation, a national manpower commission and an industrial court to resolve industrial litigation.

4 May Final report of the Erasmus Commission says Vorster must take blame for the Information Scandal, but clears PW Botha. Vorster resigns as President.

8 May Riekert Commission recommends more black involvement in government

administration boards, active promotion of home ownership, wider opportunities for black traders in white areas, lifting curfews on blacks in urban areas, and scrapping random pass arrests.

children under 18 of someone with such rights). But with the economic failure of the homelands, and the growing demand for jobs in a metropolitan industrial sector depleted of white blue-collar workers and expanding in excess of the existing labour provision, racial constraints on employment gave in.

This did not mean, though, that natural economic and social processes were allowed free play. The failures of policy were compounded by their more vigorous implementation. Typical of the heartless procedure was the displacement of 10 000 'illegal' black residents in the midwinter destruction of the Modderdam settlement on the Cape Flats in 1977. A journalist described such 'squatter clearance' as 'an eye-smarting hell of teargas and snarling dogs, of laughing officials and policemen, of homeless families crouched pitifully with their meagre possessions beside the road'.

Reaffirming Great Trek mythology, Prime Minister PW Botha signs miniature *vierkleur* – old Boer republic – flags for children at Day of the Vow celebrations in Heidelberg on 16 December 1980.

17 May Advocate General Bill seeks to block publication of information on alleged state fraud; widely condemned as a 'totalitarian measure' and 'press gag'.

June Congress of South African Students is formed.

July Secretary of Health announces that all senior public service doctors, whatever their race, will be paid the same.

August Botha draws up a comprehensive national strategy, reappraising the apartheid policy and reiterating his aim of establishing a constellation of independent African states. He announces a 12-point plan at the NP congress on 15 August.

31 August Botha becomes the first South African prime minister to visit Soweto.

Two years later, fastidious officials were tracking down 'illegals' in the suburbs. In human terms, the costs of the failing policy were high. A cameo from the heart of suburban Cape Town – recounted in a letter to a newspaper by a Newlands housewife – conveyed the irrationality and profound indignity of the enterprise:

Recently the Bantu Administration Inspectors did a raid in the Claremont/Newlands area. They picked up women coming back from church and shopping. Some were pushed around to try and force them to tell the names of their employers and where they lived. They spent the night, before appearing in court the next morning, on a bare and dirty cement floor … with nothing to eat or drink, including no water, with just one bucket as a latrine for 30 women … These women are in the Western Cape because they have to work to feed and educate their families in the Transkei. They will all vouch that there is no work for them in the Transkei. They are honest and loyal. They work in our homes and look after our children. How long must these women go on living in fear because they happen to be working honestly, and then fined R50 or 50 days in jail for doing so?

The flooding of the cities by work-seekers fleeing the Bantustans, which the government may have viewed as a crisis of black defiance, was the symptom of a deeper crisis, the crisis of apartheid's fundamental unviability.

While Transkei leader Kaiser Matanzima went on grandly in 1980 about the virtues of his so-called independence – 'to be free makes you able to do things you would not do while you were not free' – a contemporary account of neighbouring Ciskei presented a truer image: a 'tiny piece of land … with the highest population density in South Africa', a 'vast ghetto', overgrazed and crammed with people who couldn't get out except as contract workers, a desolate countryside in which one would 'come to a settlement of tens of thousands of people, a township without a town … with no visible means of life support.'

Economically, the logic of the homeland system was decrepit. Helen Suzman pointed out that while a job could be created in the metropolitan areas for about R9 000, it didn't make sense trying to create the same job in an industry deliberately set up on the edge of a remote homeland when the cost was four times higher at R36 000. In KwaZulu, Mangosuthu Buthelezi, who opted for limited self-rule, resisted 'independence' on the grounds that 'our people realise they can

3 September Dr Frederik van Zyl Slabbert succeeds Colin Eglin as leader of the Progressive Federal Party.
13 September South Africa proclaims Venda 'independent'.

November Government announces a plan to allow white and black businessmen to form partnerships as part of a strategy to draw blacks into free enterprise.

10 December Group Areas Act permit system is relaxed for a wide range of shared facilities, including libraries, private hospitals, restaurants, theatres, concerts, exhibitions, and drive-in cinemas.

only maximise their rights in the labour market if they remain South Africans,' but the sort of opinion Nationalists liked to hear was that of Bophuthatswana's Lucas Mangope, that 'independence has enhanced the self-esteem of the people, it has created self-reliance'.

PW Botha fostered these illusions as he moved to give substance to his fine-sounding sentiments about acknowledging people's rights and 'making ourselves free by giving to others in a spirit of justice what we demand for ourselves'. It was a process that was increasingly difficult to control, not least because of the far-reaching impact of two government commissions in the late 1970s. The Wiehahn Commission's convincing argument that formal labour

Family life was denied to migrant workers, like these men photographed in Mamelodi, Pretoria, in 1989. This workers' hostel was typical of the mean accommodation built for homeland 'citizens' who, while indispensable to the economy, had no rights of permanent residence.

1980

ANC declares 1980 the Year of the Charter, marking the 25th anniversary of the adoption of the Freedom Charter in 1955.

February The army takes over security of northern Natal.

21 February South Africa warns Mozambique it will not hesitate to strike back if Mozambique continues to shelter guerrillas.

29 February Justice Petrus Cillié's final report on the Soweto uprising says imposition of Afrikaans as the language of tuition

was the immediate cause of the protest, compounded by 'underlying dissatisfaction'.

March *Sunday Post* launches a nationwide 'Release Mandela' campaign; some 15 million sign the petition.

WORKERS OF THE WORLD

Workers of South Africa unite in the 1985 launch of the Congress of South African Trade Unions (COSATU), opening a new front in the fight against apartheid.

rights be extended to black workers and the Riekert Commission's proposals that black workers be given more freedom to choose where to work resulted in a mushrooming of black union activity. In most instances, this was inseparable from political activism, especially after the formation of the half-million-strong Congress of South African Trade Unions (COSATU) in 1985, and the scrapping of the pass laws in 1986.

The findings of an earlier commission influenced government thinking on constitutional reform. In 1976, the Theron Commission's advice that coloured

9 March Botha says all races will take part in a constitutional conference, but he rejects one man, one vote.

April-July Extensive boycotts and disruption at schools and universities; more than 30 die in police action.

1 April Nine southern African countries meet in Lusaka to form the Southern African Development Coordination Conference (SADCC) to promote regional development and lessen dependence on South Africa.

18 April Zimbabwe gains independence.

8 May Government accepts Schlebusch Commission recommendation to replace Senate with a President's Council of 60 whites, coloureds, Indians and Chinese (but no blacks).

people be given a more direct say in government coincided with the Soweto uprising, and was rejected at the time, perhaps in part because of the pupils' revolt. Once PW Botha got into his stride, however, the idea of giving limited political say to coloured and Indian people – matching black self-government in the Bantustans – was an attractive option that meshed with his thinking about a 'total strategy' to create a moderate bulwark against what he characterised as the 'total onslaught' of revolutionaries – everybody from guerrillas and their allies in the frontline states (and the Soviet Union) to school, labour and community activists, and protesters and organisers of sanctions and boycotts abroad. He hoped to use the scrapping of petty apartheid measures, such as race barriers at theatres, cinemas and restaurants, to lighten the burden of grievance on those who would gladly participate in modest political reforms – and be rewarded for their trouble – while using whatever means were necessary to 'neutralise' or 'eliminate' the graver threats. Thus, security concerns were placed at the centre of civilian government. Botha's 'total strategy' provided for, and became largely driven by, a National Security Management System, which subordinated policy-making to security considerations, and was dominated by so-called securocrats attuned more to risk than opportunity.

By 1980, the momentum of change, and the scale of risks, was mounting. Zimbabwe became independent under former guerrilla leader Robert Mugabe, and the principle, if not yet all the details, of Namibian independence was accepted. The armed struggle was more palpable on home ground; the June 1980 bomb attack on the Sasol oil-from-coal plant, though it hardly dented the economy, stimulated anxiety about South Africa's vulnerability, not least because the plant itself was a response to international hostility and the risk of the oil embargo's stifling the country's economic lifeline. Agitation for the release of Nelson Mandela became more prominent with the launching of the Free Mandela campaign by Bishop Desmond Tutu, general secretary of the South African Council of Churches. The atmosphere of resistance was everywhere reinforced by waves of protests and boycotts.

In these conditions, Botha began to elaborate his 12-point plan, unveiled in 1979, whose key elements were a new constitution, recognising the rights of ethnic groups, removing 'unnecessary discrimination' and creating a 'constellation

---

1 **June** Umkhonto we Sizwe strikes at the Sasol 1 complex at Sasolburg, causing damage estimated at R66 million. A second limpet mine strike at Sasol II at Secunda fails. ANC president Oliver Tambo confirms both attacks are the work of guerrilla units.

23 **July** Botha announces a Constellation Committee to promote his concept of a 'constellation of Southern African states'.
31 **October** Draft laws are gazetted to give blacks greater mobility and security of tenure in white areas.

23 **December** *Post Transvaal*, *Saturday Post* and *Sunday Post* newspapers are banned on a technicality.

of southern African states'. The whole package was predicated on gradual change and the maintenance of security – in effect, the quelling of resistance.

The creation of a President's Council in 1980 to replace the Senate indicated more the limits than the potential reach of the Botha administration's idea of reform. The new body, which was asked to suggest a new form of government, was made up of nominated white, coloured and Indian representatives, but excluded blacks entirely. For conservatives, it went too far; for credible black leaders, it fell far too short of the minimum requirement for meaningful discussion. If there was any doubt about international sentiment, it was dispelled in the early 1980s.

Far from winning any significant encouragement from the Western powers, the Botha administration's constitutional tinkering – including expunging almost 800 discriminatory provisions from legislation – attracted yet more repudiation in the form of a blacklist of apartheid 'collaborators' covering every sphere from sport and entertainment to arms. And, when the Springboks set off for New Zealand in 1981, on what turned out to be their last and most controversial tour for years, violent encounters with protesters earned greater attention than clashes on the field. One of the most effective campaigns of the time was built on the South African Council on Sport (SACOS) slogan 'No normal sport in an abnormal society'. White South Africa's enthusiasm for equality on the sports field, but not at the ballot box, no longer counted for much.

The fissures in parliamentary politics were revealed in the results of the 1981 general election; the Nationalists still won with the landslide performance they'd become accustomed to, taking 131 of the 165 seats, but now with losses to left and right. The Progressive Federal Party – led since 1979 by the assured young Afrikaner Frederik van Zyl Slabbert – increased its share to 26 seats. The right-wing Herstigte Nasionale Party, which, because it was always contesting NP seats, struggled to get into Parliament at all, nevertheless grew its support from an unremarkable 39 500 votes in 1974 to more than 192 300 in 1981.

United Democratic Front (UDF) affiliates at an August 1984 rally endorse demands for the release of long-jailed ANC leader Nelson Mandela.

1981

9 January Draft legislation is published allowing hotels and restaurants to admit blacks.

14 January A proposed amendment to the Population Registration Act will make fingerprinting of all races – and a uniform indentity document – compulsory.

30 January SADF kills 12 claimed ANC members in raids on Matolo, Mozambique.

2 February A new daily paper, the *Sowetan*, is launched to replace the banned *Post* titles.

20 March KwaNdebele proclaimed a self-governing territory.

20 April A bomb explosion at a power station near Durban causes an extensive blackout and temporarily paralyses industry in the area. It is attributed to the ANC.

29 April National Party's majority slightly reduced in general election.

12 August ANC claims responsibility for a rocket attack on the Voortrekkerhoogte military complex in Pretoria.

August Protests in Cape Town over the forced removal of people from Nyanga camp.

8 October HSRC report recommends the opening of white government schools to blacks, but government affirms commitment to segregated education.

3 December Ciskei becomes 'independent'. Lennox Sebe is elected president.

29 December Winnie Mandela is banned for a further five years and continues to be restricted to Brandfort.

In the aftermath of the Soweto uprising, thousands of young South Africans left the country to join Umkhonto we Sizwe. Here, four new recruits - from left, Elsie Biki (15), her brother Ernest (17), Michael Simango (17) and Richard Gardiner (16) - are interviewed by journalist Abdulla Riyama soon after their arrival in Tanzania.

The big break for the Afrikaner right came a little less than a year later when 16 rebel MPs of the *verkrampte*, or hardline, section of the ruling party were ousted over their implacable opposition to reform, and banded together as the Conservative Party (CP) under Andries Treurnicht, the former Deputy Minister of Bantu Education whose infamous mishandling of the crisis over forced Afrikaans tuition in black schools prompted the 1976 Soweto uprising. But politics was no longer principally about what happened or what was said in Parliament. The government itself deepened the growing irrelevance of parliamentary oversight by engaging in wide-ranging extrajudicial activity and reaching beyond the borders to pursue its sovereign goals on foreign soil.

Tens of thousands of South Africans were living in exile by the early 1980s, chiefly across Europe and North America, and in various centres in Africa.

1982

8 January At a gathering in Dar es Salaam, Tanzania, to celebrate the 70th anniversary of the ANC's founding, Oliver Tambo declares that 1982 will be a year of massive actions against apartheid.

11 January UN Special Committee against Apartheid launches the International Year of Mobilisation for Sanctions against South Africa.

1 February Justice Marthinus Steyn's Commission of Inquiry into the media recommends a general council of journalists to regulate entry into the profession and judge journalists accused of violating a statutory code of conduct.

Among them were legions of Umkhonto we Sizwe combatants. A feature of the post-1976 political terrain was that while MK had grown to between 6 000 and 10 000 fighters, the bulk of its soldiers languished in training camps and bases in Angola, Zambia and other countries, while, with a few notable exceptions, the struggle was fought on home ground by activists who lacked military training. South Africa's geographical and logistical constraints, and the ruthless sophistication of its armed forces and intelligence and informer networks, militated against any large-scale deployment by the ANC of militia forces. On the other hand, the ANC's own commitment to avoiding civilian deaths, or terror, limited its options; as the 1980s wore on, though, commanders became less squeamish on this point, and not least because South Africa's generals increasingly did not distinguish civilians from combatants, or political opposition from military threat.

Yet MK posed a sufficient threat to attract military as well unconventional strikes on its bases and cells in neighbouring states. Hit squads and agents of the so-called Civil Cooperation Bureau and other agencies undertook missions ranging from scaring people to killing them in cold blood. In 1982, a lethal covert operation claimed the life of activist and author Ruth First – wife of leading communist and ANC strategist Joe Slovo – when she opened a letter bomb sent to her office at the Centre for African Studies at Maputo's Eduardo Mondlane University. A car bomb killed Petrus Nzima, the ANC's representative in Mbabane, Swaziland, along with his wife, Jabu. In the first week of December, the South African Defence Force (SADF) 'hit' 12 targets in the residential suburbs of Lesotho's capital, Maseru, killing 41, including women and children. A newspaper report the next day quoting an unnamed South African exile in Maseru described the 'terror, devastation and death' of the night-time raid, 'as helicopters roared overhead and gunfire and explosions ripped the night apart'. The deaths of five women and two children in the attacks were confirmed by the South African authorities, who 'regretted that the innocent had also had to suffer'.

Both sides invariably argued – as combatants in ideological conflicts usually do – that there were no innocents. This was certainly the case when, some six months later, the ANC retaliated for the Maseru attack. A news report from Pretoria on 21 May 1983 conveyed a vivid picture of the aftermath of the

5 February Detained trade unionist Dr Neil Aggett is found dead in his cell at security police headquarters in Johannesburg. On 11 February more than 85 000 workers join a work stoppage in protest. An inquest finds no one is to blame for Aggett's death.

24 February Twenty-two dissident Nationalist MPs oppose Botha, and are given eight days to recant. On 2 March Andries Treurnicht resigns as Minister of State Administration and Statistics and announces the formation of the Conservative Party, with 16 MPs.

14 March A bomb wrecks the ANC offices in Islington, London.

14 March Botha spells out a new constitutional dispensation for coloureds and Indians in radio and television interviews.

late-afternoon car bomb outside the downtown headquarters of the South African Air Force, which killed 19 – including the two MK operatives in the vehicle – and wounded 200:

> *A body flung right through heavy wooden doors, glass-covered pavements, wrecked cars and a pair of high-heeled shoes standing neatly in a pool of blood. These are some of the scenes from the horrifying bomb explosion yesterday. Some of the young policemen gagged as they passed pool after pool of blood. Elsewhere, someone stumbled over a toddler's gumboot. Stacked against the entrance to Nedbank Square were blood-spattered handbags, briefcases, shoes and clothing.*

The official reaction was predictably – or even understandably – bellicose. Defence minister Magnus Malan said the government 'would not hesitate to launch more Maseru-style pre-emptive attacks on ANC bases to prevent further atrocities', while Prime Minister PW Botha declared: 'This act confirms once again that we are dealing with a communist-inspired assault of great intensity in which there will be no hesitation to kill even innocent people.' Botha seemed to overlook his own forces' scant hesitation in killing innocent people in just such 'Maseru-style pre-emptive attacks'.

Towards the end of 1983, fear, and perhaps also a little hope, inspired white voters to turn out in big numbers in a referendum on a new constitution, to give Botha's reform plans a firm thumbs up. The 66% 'yes' vote cleared the way for the new three-chamber, or tricameral, Parliament that would give coloureds and Indians a role in government, but exclude black people. Most whites regarded it as a step in the right direction, away from the politics of violence. Conservatives saw it as capitulation, but were not alone in opposing it. Progressive Federal Party leader Frederik van Zyl Slabbert and Harry Oppenheimer, chairman of the giant Anglo American Corporation and one of the country's most influential businessmen, were among prominent liberals who campaigned against the tricameral set-up, warning that blacks would bitterly resent being excluded once more.

Tricameralism was much mocked for its bewildering constitutional architecture and wasteful duplication, and for the disingenuous euphemisms that barely obscured its truer purpose. Its master interpreter, Minister of Constitutional

---

23 March Military call-up expanded to include all white men between 17 and 65. Commando units to be strengthened.
28 March Armscor announces production of a world-beating 155mm artillery system, the G5 gun.

1 April Nelson Mandela, Walter Sisulu, Raymond Mhlaba and Andrew Mlangeni are moved from Robben Island to Pollsmoor prison. A few months later they are joined by Ahmed Kathrada.

30 April Zambian president Kenneth Kaunda meets Botha on the Botswana border to discuss the political situation in Namibia and South Africa. This is the first meeting between any leader of a frontline state and a South African premier since August 1976.

25c
(24c + 1c GST)

CAPE TOWN, MONDAY MAY 23 1983

LATE
FINAL

Traffic stops, pedestrians run for cover as SA jets attack Mozambique

ANC blasted in Maputo

General Malan

Argus Correspondent

TRAFFIC in Maputo stopped and pedestrians dived for cover as South African Air Force jets blasted six ANC bases in a dawn raid on Mozambique today.

Manuela Ferreira of the Portuguese news agency, Noticias de Portugal, said ground forces answered the attacking jets "with what sounded like machine-gun fire."

No immediate details of casualties or damage were available, but it was believed to have been extensive. All the South African aircraft returned to base safely.

In what was clearly a retaliatory raid following the Pretoria bomb blast, the jets attacked:

● A FAM (Mozambique Defence Force) missile site which protected the targets.
● The headquarters of the Transvaal urban "machinery" of the ANC responsible for the actions in Transvaal urban areas.
● The headquarters of the ANC's Transvaal rural 'machinery'.
● The command post from which sabotage orders were issued.
● The training centre where ANC members were taught to handle limpet mines, weaponry and explosives.
● A logistical headquarters and supply point.

The SAAF strike came between 7 and 8 am today while clearing up operations were still in progress in Pretoria.

Still in progress

Announcing the raid, the Minister of Defence, General Magnus Malan, said a Mozambique armed forces missile site protecting the target area was "neutralised".

He added that although the retaliatory attack could "never compensate for the cowardly car bomb attack . . . in Pretoria, it would at least demonstrate to the world and South Africa's enemies that South Africa was ready to act where and when necessary"

Ammo depot struck

MAPUTO. — A South African civil aviation official said today an office block was flattened and an ammunition depot blown up in the air raid here.

A Western diplomat in Maputo confirmed the attack on the city by South African warplanes.

The diplomat said witnesses saw jets fly overhead and a cloud of smoke in an area called Liberdad.

The diplomat said President Samora Machel's Government appeared to have moved most ANC activities to the north of the country, out of reach of South African planes.

ANC strategist Joe Slovo, who plans most of the ANC's sabotage attacks, had been in and out of Maputo in recent months, added the diplomat.

Last year, Slovo's wife, Ruth First, was killed by a letter-bomb sent to her university office in Maputo, allegedly by South Africa.

The diplomat rejected the South African claim that Mozambican forces were providing a defence umbrella for the ANC. — Sapa-AP.

IN THE aftermath of the horrors of the car bomb explosion, Pretoria businessman Mr Bill Zurich counts the money

The weather:
Cool

SOUTH AFRICAN Pieter Schoeman, left, and Portuguese Gomes Leitao were among a group of prisoners paraded at a mass open-air rally, attended by 50 000, in Maputo on Saturday.

ITS facade shredded by the blast of the bomb, the Nedbank building in Church Street was just one of those with smashed windows, cracked masonry and damaged shopfronts.

The anti-apartheid insurgency aimed at the heart of Nationalist power in its 1983 car bomb attack in central Pretoria (left) gave critics reason to call its strategy 'terror'. Days after the devastating blast in Pretoria, newspaper headlines trumpeted the retaliatory attacks launched by the South African Air Force on ANC bases in Mozambique (above). The ANC always argued that the aggression began with apartheid itself.

6 May Botha announces that eight Western intelligence agents, held by the Soviet Union, and one South African soldier, held in Angola, have been exchanged somewhere in Europe for Major AM Kozlov, a senior Soviet intelligence officer arrested in South Africa in July 1980.

12 May President's Council recommends a degree of power-sharing between the white, coloured and Indian communities at central government level, and for blacks only at local government level.

17 August Activist and writer Dr Ruth First is killed by a letter bomb in Maputo.

9 December South African forces raid houses in Maseru, Lesotho, killing 30 members of the ANC, as well as women and children.

18 December Four explosions occur at the Koeberg nuclear power station, outside Cape Town, for which the ANC claims responsibility.

Development Chris Heunis, once baldly asserted that it was designed to 'accommodate the coloured people and Indians without detracting from the self-determination of the whites'. A bemused public was left to ponder such impenetrable concepts as 'vertical differentiation with the built-in principle of self-determination … [achieved] on as many levels as possible'.

Coloured and Indian MPs (and white ones, in their separate chamber) were left more or less to their own devices on so-called 'own affairs' matters – such as education, culture, local government and health – while 'general affairs' policy-making on defence, foreign affairs, justice and police required approval from all three chambers. The risk of any truly reformist enthusiasm among the new MPs was thus neutralised. Presiding over all was newly elevated State President Botha, the executive head of government and commander-in-chief of the armed forces.

A pitifully low turnout of 30% of registered coloured voters and 20% of Indians delivered a result in August 1984 which gave Allan Hendrickse's Labour Party control of the (coloured) House of Representatives, and Amichand Rajbansi's National People's Party control of the (Indian) House of Delegates. That the new system reinforced the unforgiving error of the 1910 Union constitution – the exclusion of the black majority – was the fundamental flaw that no amount of fine-sounding sentiment could overcome.

Yet there were meaningful consequences. Life and work in Parliament underwent a telling change. Former president FW de Klerk recalled of the tricameral era that there was 'genuine political interaction and accountability', with white Cabinet ministers having to report to coloured and Indian MPs and being 'exposed to criticism and indignation over the injustices of apartheid'. Sometimes ministers were 'shouted down and had to listen to moving protestations and views that they had never before experienced or heard so directly'. The result of such interaction 'broadened the attitudes of all those involved'.

An unintended consequence, as journalist Brian Lapping pointed out, was that for all their deficiencies, Botha's reform 'innovations' meant that the government 'could hardly ban political campaigning. It had created the legal space for its opponents to manoeuvre.'

Civil society lost no time in exploiting the opportunity to argue that there was no merit in fighting for change within the system when the system itself

1983

May Government announces plans to build a new township, Khayelitsha, in the Cape Peninsula. This is a major policy reversal, acknowledging the permanence of black residents in the Cape.

20 May Nineteen people are killed and more than 200 injured in a car bomb explosion outside air force headquarters in Pretoria.
23 May Six people are killed and more than 30 injured in South African Air Force retaliatory raid on Maputo.

30 May Appeal Court hands down landmark decision in the case of Rikhoto vs East Rand Administration Board, granting the plaintiff the right to permanent urban status. This ruling meant that 150 000 black contract workers in urban areas could now apply to have their families live with them.

Not for real, the cartoonist suggests: South Africa's brief tricameral episode doubtless nudged some whites towards reformist thinking, but the exclusion of blacks guaranteed its failure.

had to go. In early 1983, activist and cleric Allan Boesak, then president of the World Alliance of Reformed Churches, told a meeting of the Indian Congress in Johannesburg that working within the system 'contaminates you'. Engaging in compromise for the sake of politics 'is in fact selling out your principles, your ideals and the future of your children'. Setting out the vision of an alliance of organisations coalescing to confront 'the system' head-on, Boesak suggested that 'churches, civic organisations, trade unions, student organisations and sports bodies should unite on this issue … [and] inform the people of the fraud that is about to be perpetrated in their name'.

Precisely such an amalgam of forces was formed at a clamorous meeting at a civic hall in Cape Town's sprawling coloured satellite suburb of Mitchells Plain on 20 August 1983. Boesak, one of its prominent founders, earned a roar of

12 June National Forum, representing 170 black organisations, holds its first conference at Hammanskraal and adopts a manifesto identifying racial capitalism as the real enemy and pledging to establish a socialist republic.

20 August United Democratic Front (UDF) is launched in Mitchells Plain, opposing the government's constitutional proposals and pledging support for a single non-racial and unfragmented South Africa.

September Republic of South African Constitution Act provides for a state president with wide-ranging executive powers and a tricameral parliament. The law is approved in Parliament by 119 to 35 votes.

approval from the more than 10 000 people packed into the hall and a marquee alongside when he defined the objective of the United Democratic Front (UDF) in three words: 'all, here and now … we want all our rights, we want them here and we want them now'. A similar front, the Black Consciousness-inspired National Forum, was launched by the Azanian People's Organisation (AZAPO) and other groups, including the socialist Cape Action League, at a meeting at Hammanskraal, near Pretoria, two months earlier. But it was the UDF that seized activists and succeeded in embodying – and, to a large extent, organising – the struggle. And, given its discrete, non-racial and agglomerated form, the UDF was not easily isolated or neutralised. Within months, it incorporated some 600 civic and student organisations and unions, boasting an estimated membership of three million.

The scale of resistance was tragically heightened by a measure through which the government had wrongly calculated it might appease and co-opt an emergent urban black middle class: the granting of semi-autonomous local government in townships. Urbanisation had grown dramatically from the late 1970s, and with it a vigorous ideological consciousness and street-level political organisation. The sop of municipal reform only inflamed sentiments, and black anger erupted in violence.

On the very day of the tricameral Parliament's first sitting on 3 September 1984, Sharpeville earned headlines once more when its newly elected deputy mayor was hacked to death on his doorstep, two people were burned to death trapped in their cars, four were strangled behind a plundered garage, and a man was burned to death in a liquor store. Black people regarded as collaborators were mercilessly slain. In many cases, candidates for local councils were too scared to stand. If such fear was strategically successful, excesses of violence damaged the black cause – especially the emergence of the dreaded 'necklace' used to murder people often only suspected of being collaborators. The grim term referred to a petrol-soaked tyre placed over the head of a victim – whose hands were bound – and set alight. This ruthless procedure was ingloriously, if only rhetorically, exploited by Winnie Mandela two years later when she told a rally: 'Together, hand in hand, with our boxes of matches and our necklaces we shall liberate this country.'

26 October UN Special Committee Against Apartheid publishes a register of entertainers, actors and others who have performed in South Africa.

2 November In a referendum, whites (65.9%) approve new tricameral constitution.

5 December A bomb explosion, shattering the Johannesburg office of the Department of Foreign Affairs, is the 42nd attack by ANC saboteurs in 1983.

14 December South Africa invades Angola on the pretext of attacking SWAPO bases.

1984

8 January South African forces begin withdrawal from southern Angola.

14 March Koeberg nuclear power station becomes operational.

Nelson Mandela, whose imprisonment had become the focal point of the international campaign against apartheid, was evidently perceived within Botha's inner circle as the key to calming the country, but they misjudged his fortitude and his principles. When, in January 1985, PW Botha announced that he would free Mandela if the ANC leader 'unconditionally rejected violence as a political instrument', the excitement about this seeming concession was short-lived. Mandela's reply, read in public by his daughter Zindzi in February, was a statement of moving conviction, electrifying not least because this was the first time in more than 20 years that South Africans had heard him 'speak'.

National freedom, he said in his statement, was the core issue. 'I am not less life-loving than you are. But I cannot sell my birthright, nor am I prepared to sell

Cleric Allan Boesak articulates the popular rejection of the tricameral constitution at the launch of the United Democratic Front (UDF) in Cape Town in August 1983.

16 March Mozambican president Samora Machel and Botha sign the Nkomati Accord, a non-aggression pact.

1 April Black Communities Development Act introduces freehold ownership, with conditions.

April Carnegie Report on Poverty in South Africa reveals that the number of blacks living below the poverty line doubled between 1960 and 1980.

11 May Release of longest-serving white political prisoner, David Kitson, seven

months short of completing his 20-year sentence for sabotage.

May South Africa concedes that almost 2 million black people have been relocated since 1960.

the birthright of the people to be free ... Only free men can negotiate. Prisoners cannot enter into contracts ... I cannot and will not give any undertaking at a time when I and you, the people, are not free.' Mandela's assured stand emboldened activists. For the government, it was an unpromising start to the year. But things got much worse.

A month later, a protest march in Uitenhage's Langa township to mark the 25th anniversary of the Sharpeville massacre came to a bloody end when police opened fire, killing 20. World condemnation was matched by fury in South Africa – and, increasingly, resistance by young whites. Conscripted troops, deployed in townships since October in the previous year, were deployed in ever-greater numbers after the Langa catastrophe. Disquiet among soldiers, encouraged by the 1984 launch of the End Conscription Campaign, turned to open defiance.

These developments were watched with interest from Lusaka, the ANC's base since the late 1960s. Under very different circumstances at its first consultative conference at Morogoro, Tanzania, in 1969, the ANC had agreed in principle to admit white members. At its second conference, at Kabwe, Zambia, in 1985, it voted overwhelmingly in favour of open membership, articulating the strengthening of white support as a tactical goal, and urging whites to decide where they stood.

The government, on the other hand, was mired in its crisis. Nothing it did seemed to have any meaningful effect, either in reducing tension, giving critics pause or even simply keeping the lid on revolt. A sense of pathos, almost, accompanied the announcement in April that the Prohibition of Mixed Marriages Act and the sex-across-the-colour-bar clause of the Immorality Act were to be scrapped, as if these really mattered now, or could be taken as meaningful signs in the setting of

A South African Defence Force patrol in Imbali township, Pietermaritzburg, an 'unrest' measure common in townships across the country from the second half of 1984.

29 May to 12 June Botha visits eight countries in Europe - Portugal, Great Britain, West Germany, Belgium, France, Austria, Italy and Switzerland - and has an audience with Pope John Paul II. The tour is seen in South Africa as a diplomatic breakthrough, signalling the end of isolation.

30 May Group Areas Amendment Act declares certain central business districts free trade areas.
28 June In Lubango, Angola, exiled South African Jenny Schoon and her daughter Katryn are killed by a parcel bomb, probably

intended for her husband Marius Schoon, who was named in security trials as an agent of the ANC.
12 July Car bomb explosion in Durban kills five and injures twenty-six.

136 APARTHEID: AN ILLUSTRATED HISTORY

horrific bloodshed that impelled the government in July to impose a state of emergency in 36 magisterial districts. Within days, ANC leader Oliver Tambo called for a groundswell of resistance to make South Africa 'ungovernable'; the economic crisis deepened with stiffer sanctions and a fall in credit ratings, and several European countries recalled their ambassadors.

As in 1960, the last time the government had resorted to emergency measures, the mid-1980s called for an imaginative and decisive political response, which, in fact, some key figures in the party believed was possible and desirable. But could Botha deliver it? Encouraged by reform-minded ministers such as Pik Botha at Foreign Affairs and Chris Heunis at Constitutional Development, the National

Nelson Mandela's daughter, Zindzi, is feted at a UDF rally in Durban in February 1985. In the same month she read in public her father's rejection of the government's offer to release him conditionally.

22 August Elections to the House of Representatives (for coloured voters) show overwhelming support for the Labour Party. Official results record only a 30.9% turnout.

28 August Elections to the House of Delegates (for Indian voters) show most

support for the National People's Party. Elections marked by a low poll and protests.

3 September Violence greets the inauguration of the tricameral Parliament. Violence, protests and extensive boycotts continue for months.

17 November Opposition PFP opens its membership to all races, despite the Prohibition of Political Interference Act which forbids mixed political parties. It also opposes conscription now that the army is being used to suppress unrest. The decision draws strong opposition within the party.

Sheena Duncan of the Black Sash and activist Anton Lubowski (right) endorse the End Conscription Campaign demands for the withdrawal of troops from Namibia at a 1984 press conference.

Party began to look seriously at fundamental changes to ease the crisis at home and gain credit abroad. In outline – necessarily, there were no details – the vision involved common citizenship, including black leaders in the Cabinet as well as in a constitutional forum, and scrapping more discriminatory laws. It would be a bold statement of intent, and the obvious opportunity to deliver it was the annual National Party conference in Durban on 15 August 1985. In the preceding two weeks, however, the reformists' idea that South Africa was ready to 'cross the Rubicon' and a recalcitrant President Botha's conservative and suspicious inclinations parted company.

There is no final account of why the crushing letdown of Botha's hectoring 15 August speech occurred, but a combination of factors evidently convinced him to pull back from offering the prospect of a major shift. A frenzy of media speculation in the weeks before the speech – typical of which was *Time* magazine's anticipation of the 'most important announcement since the Dutch settlers arrived

---

21 November Demonstrations begin outside the South African embassy in Washington, DC, and continue almost daily.

10 December US President Ronald Reagan calls on Pretoria to engage in effective dialogue with blacks to address the aspirations of all South Africans.

1985

10 February Nelson Mandela turns down offer of release by Botha on 31 January.

18 February Arrests of top UDF leaders. Of the thirteen detained, six are to be charged with high treason.

21 February Government announces 99-year leasehold rights for blacks in three Cape Town townships in a bid to quell resistance over forced removals.

in South Africa 300 years ago' – raised expectations, perhaps unreasonably. So did Foreign minister Pik Botha's enthusiastic briefings to European and American leaders and diplomats just before the Durban conference.

It might be that PW Botha was wise enough to see that nothing he could offer would match either these new expectations or the demands of the only rival that really mattered – the ANC. And the West was already decided on adding pressure. At the end of July, responding to criticism and deposit with-drawals by anti-apartheid students, churches and charities, the big American bank, Chase Manhattan – which, like other banks, had long ignored protests – refused to renew a South African loan. Without substantial international loans, the country couldn't sustain either high white living standards or the economic growth required to absorb the dramatic increase of black job-seekers entering the urban labour market.

At the eleventh hour, Botha decided to write his own speech, discarding the one party reformists had spent weeks helping to craft. And when he stood to address party, country and a world audience of more than 200 million, the president came across not as a statesman turning away from the disaster of apartheid, but, in historian Hermann Giliomee's estimation, as the finger-wagging 'stereo-type of the ugly, irredeemable Afrikaner'. Even as he stuck to the now hollow Rubicon metaphor, Botha told the world: 'Don't push us too far.' He would not lead whites or other minorities to 'abdication and suicide'.

The reaction of the West was swift and sharp: other major banks followed Chase Manhattan's lead, compelling the government to impose a four-month freeze on foreign debt repayments; capital fled; the rand fell; and, in late August, the US Congress approved the Comprehensive Anti-Apartheid Act, prohibiting new loans and investment, withdrawing landing rights and curbing coal, uran-ium, iron and steel imports. The Commonwealth and the European Community followed suit with other sanctions.

To mass unemployment was added rising costs; in the year to December 1985, inflation ran at 18.4%, its highest level in 66 years. South Africa was militarily robust, but economically vulnerable, and a strident international campaign for sanctions against apartheid, emphatically endorsed by 1984 Nobel Peace Prize winner Bishop Desmond Tutu, was quick to exploit the moment.

---

21 March Police kill 20 marchers in Langa, Uitenhage, during a commemoration of the 25th anniversary of the Sharpeville massacre. In June, Justice Donald Kannemeyer's commission of inquiry blames the police for the events leading to the shooting.

April Government announces it will repeal Mixed Marriages Act, Prohibition of Political Interference Act and racial provisions of Immorality Act.

14 June ANC bases in Gaborone, Botswana, are attacked by South African commandos. At least 15 people are killed.

25 June At its Kabwe Conference, the ANC opens its national executive committee to all race groups, appointing five Indian, white and coloured people to the committee.

Looking back in 2008, Giliomee observed: 'Although the reforms announced in the NP's four provincial congresses in 1985 amounted to a major policy shift … [t]he Rubicon speech signals the day when the Botha government unmistakeably lost both the initiative and its credibility. In terms of security it could still hold the ring, but politically, economically and diplomatically it would not recover.'

The axis of political attention tilted for good; the ANC, still banned and silenced – and feared and reviled in much of the white establishment – was emerging all the more clearly as the next show in town.

Within a month of Botha's Rubicon fiasco, savvy businessmen and key figures in other spheres defied Botha's admonishments and flew north by the planeload to pay their respects and sound out what they knew were their future rulers on such ticklish questions as property rights and economic policy, electoral government and free speech. A 14 September news report, datelined 'Luangwa Game Park, Zambia', told how 'white South African businessmen … found enough common ground [with the ANC] to raise hopes for a solution to the country's troubles'. The six-hour talks at President Kenneth Kaunda's private lodge ended with an almost surprised Gavin Relly of Anglo American declaring that the businessmen found the ANC's attitude 'not nearly so grossly antagonistic as might be thought', and that 'we had a good sense that more talks might lead to a fruitful conclusion'.

In the weeks that followed, students, writers and others ignored official displeasure and flew to Lusaka to explore the scope for working together. It was, however, the Nationalists' iconic prisoner, Nelson Mandela, who held the real key to common-ground initiatives.

An accident of physiognomy – a prostate operation at a central Cape Town hospital towards the end of 1985 – led to Mandela's being given a cell of his own at Pollsmoor prison, the mainland jail to which he and his fellow Rivonia trialists Walter Sisulu, Ahmed Kathrada and Raymond Mhlaba had been moved from Robben Island. Here, in calm isolation, Mandela decided on his own that it was time to talk. A military victory seemed to him 'a distant if not impossible dream', pointlessly wasteful. He knew perfectly well that any decision to open negotiations 'should only have been made in Lusaka', but, even taking stock of the risk that an overture could be taken as a sign of weakness, he was convinced that 'someone from our side needed to take the first step'. And he took it.

2 July Constitutional Affairs Amendment Act allows for non-racial political parties.

5 July Two white medical doctors are found guilty of misconduct by the Medical Council in the 1977 death of Steve Biko. In October,

Dr Benjamin Tucker is struck off the roll for 'disgraceful conduct' in the affair.

20 July State of emergency declared in 36 magisterial districts.

August US imposes limited sanctions against South Africa.

15 August Botha fails to 'cross the Rubicon' in hardline speech to NP's Natal congress.

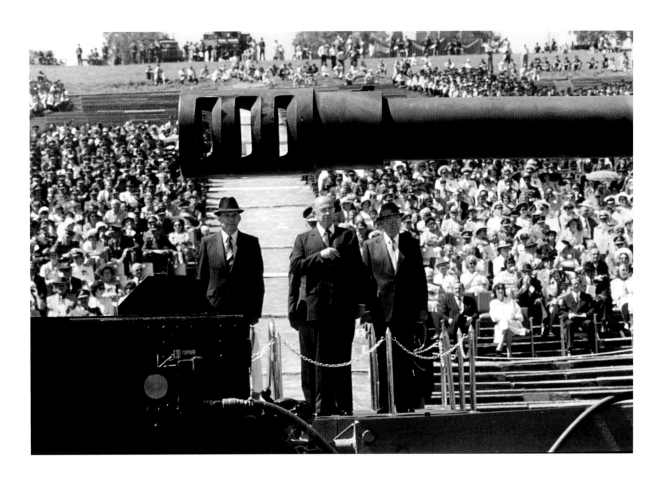

'I chose to tell no one what I was about to do,' Mandela wrote later. 'Not my colleagues upstairs (Sisulu, Kathrada and Mhlaba), nor those in Lusaka.' He knew his fellow prisoners would oppose him, but believed: 'There are times when a leader must move out ahead of his flock … confident that he is leading his people the right way.' The South African future would seem intractable for some years still, but Mandela's secret, dramatic initiative was decisive.

PW Botha's ascendance brought the country to a crisis it would take other men to resolve. In 1985, his remark seven years earlier that apartheid 'is a recipe for permanent conflict' seemed deeply ironic. Not only by default, however, he had helped fashion conditions in which a different future became inevitable. But it was the Botha administration's fate to be captive to its most famous prisoner. And Nelson Mandela was the key to a new way, the only possible source of optimism.

President PW Botha takes the salute at a Republic Day parade as the apartheid state's formidable firepower rolls by.

16 August Tambo calls for intensification of armed struggle with a view to making South Africa ungovernable.
September South Africa suspends repayment of its short-term debts.

9 October SADF chief General Constand Viljoen admits on television that the military, without government authority, has flouted the Nkomati Accord by supporting RENAMO, FRELIMO's opponents in Mozambique.

13 October PFP meets the ANC in Lusaka and calls for the release of Nelson Mandela.

CHAPTER FIVE

The rapprochement

1986-94

A new flag, and a new spirit, are on display as patriots celebrate South Africa's democratic touchdown, cramming the terraces below Pretoria's Union Buildings for the presidential inauguration of Nelson Mandela on 10 May 1994.

A wry cartoon of the final years of apartheid's crisis features two men – white men in tropical gear, each with a rifle slung over his shoulder – occupying a raised palisade, which is densely surrounded by thousands of black stick figures. The two men are evidently oblivious of their jeopardy, for one of them has a megaphone through which he asks the besiegers: 'When are you going to realise the hopelessness of your situation?' The beleaguered condition, the delusion of power, the defiance of historical forces, never mind the sheer force of numbers – all this was true of the embattled Nationalist government of the second half of the 1980s. In fact the cartoon worked both ways, though it would have been unfashionable, and certainly controversial, to have suggested as much at the time. Writing not many years later, historian Nigel Worden put it crisply when he noted that 'the state had lost the initiative but no one else had the power to seize it.' Nobody was winning. The end seemed inevitable, but it was not obvious what the end might be.

PW Botha opened Parliament on 30 January 1986 with a speech of doubtful sentiment and blandly limited vision: apartheid was 'outdated', he would chair a national statutory council that would 'include blacks', consideration would be given to legislation on 'constitutional matters', and so on. It left the core question unaddressed, as journalist Percy Qoboza pointed out a few days later when he wrote: 'Talking and negotiating with the ANC and the PAC has become something the government cannot duck any longer. They may take [out] all the refugees they want [in] Lesotho, Botswana or Swaziland, but they will not defuse those bombs. The problem is not in those countries, but right here inside our borders.'

And within the borders of South Africa, things were a mess. The securocratic state was mercilessly inflicting itself on the lives of those who opposed it. Covert units spawned by defence and security departments combined informer networks, skilled technicians and murder squads in tracking and eliminating resistance. Activists were held, tortured, killed or 'disappeared' in circumstances which suggested the implicit approval of commanding eminences in state

---

1986

January Soweto pupils return to school in response to a call from the Soweto Parents' Crisis Committee.

25 January Sixty ANC refugees airlifted out of Lesotho.

31 January Botha offers restoration of citizenship to blacks and some involvement in decision-making.

7 February Opposition PFP leader **Frederik van** Zyl Slabbert resigns from parliamentary politics.

7 March State of emergency imposed in July 1985 is lifted.

12 March Commonwealth Eminent Persons Group meets Nelson Mandela.

security structures. Atrocities were masterminded to seem to be the work of 'the enemy'.

The agents of ungovernability in townships were no less adept in the application of indiscriminate fear and death. Added to their terror of the police, of informers and of heavily armed military patrols, township residents had also to contend with the brutal excesses of young, radical 'comrades' and of the conservative, panga-wielding vigilantes who emerged, often with state assistance and encouragement, to challenge them. Division, mistrust and summary violent 'justice' was the nightmare endured by millions of black people.

If 'the people' had the ANC's armed wing, Umkhonto we Sizwe, on their side, it was not the army of liberation they might have hoped for. Nelson

The road to a negotiated settlement was bloody, with political rivals often arming themselves with rudely fashioned 'cultural weapons', vividly on display in this crowd of mourners at the funeral of the 24 victims of the Boipatong massacre.

14 April Desmond Tutu becomes Archbishop of Cape Town and head of South Africa's Anglican community.

19 May South African forces strike alleged guerrilla targets in Zambia, Botswana and Zimbabwe.

12 June A new state of emergency is declared.

24 June British Foreign Office minister Lynda Chalker meets Oliver Tambo.

1 July Influx control restrictions lifted – passes to be replaced by a uniform identity document for all.

7 July After more than 20 years of government banning, Winnie Mandela is freed of all state-ordered restrictions.

12 August KwaNdebele 'homeland' rejects independence.

Mandela himself later described the armed struggle as having power mainly as a 'rhetorical device', a 'sign that we were actively fighting the enemy' when in fact its popularity was 'out of proportion to what it had achieved on the ground'. (The Truth and Reconciliation Commission report at the end of the 1990s found that MK, though it also played a role in supporting MPLA operations against UNITA in Angola, ended up killing fewer security force members than civilians.)

The economy was buckling under the strain of social disintegration, worker resistance, soaring inflation and tightening sanctions. White society, increasingly anxious in its growing isolation, was deluded, afraid and daily reminded of its own powerlessness. For all intents and purposes, the country had reached a stalemate.

* * *

The tenth anniversary of the Soweto uprising was a daunting commemoration: the struggle was full-blown, the answering repression brutal and uncompromising. The daily news of 16 June 1986 provided a bleak snapshot: a car bomb in Durban, violence across the country with at least 22 dead over the preceding four days, a mass stayaway, draconian emergency regulations – a national state of emergency had been declared four days earlier – and a complete ban on unrest reporting. Every item of news had to be cleared by the Bureau for Information in Pretoria. Yet in the midst of the crisis itself were signs of a dynamism that would soon begin to bear fruit.

Earlier in the year, in February, Foreign minister Pik Botha's seemingly rash admission in parliamentary debate that South Africa could have a black president revealed bolder imagining in National Party ranks. His humiliating public repudiation by President Botha counted less, confirming the impression of a president who lashed out on his own account not because he was powerful but, rather, because he was unimaginative and weak.

In the same month, Frederik van Zyl Slabbert shocked the liberal establishment by resigning as leader of the opposition and as an MP, declaring parliamentary politics under the tricameral constitution a waste of time and a contributing factor rather than a solution to the political crisis. He would soon be followed

---

16 September European Economic Community imposes sanctions against South Africa, except on coal imports.
October Comprehensive Anti-Apartheid Act adopted by the US Congress.

19 October Mozambican president Samora Machel dies in a plane crash on South African territory.
4 November Oliver Tambo leads an ANC delegation in talks with Soviet leader Mikhail Gorbachev in Moscow.

1987

8 January On the ANC's 75th anniversary, Tambo rules out negotiations with the South African government.
28 January US Secretary of State George Shultz meets Tambo in Washington, DC.

by fellow MP Alex Boraine, with whom he set up the Institute for a Democratic Alternative in South Africa (IDASA), which went on to sponsor crucial contacts between white and black nationalists.

A few months later, the most meaningful contact of all was Nelson Mandela's solo initiative in reaching across the abyss when he asked for a meeting with the Botha administration's Minister of Justice, Kobie Coetsee.

The immediate prelude to their meeting was the collapse of the Commonwealth's Eminent Persons Group (EPG) initiative in mid-May, and the imposition of emergency regulations in the second week of June. The Commonwealth initiative was a compromise agreed to by British premier Margaret Thatcher, who, like Ronald Reagan in Washington, believed in influencing change by what the Americans described as 'constructive engagement'. Most Commonwealth heads of government favoured tougher sanctions, but, when Thatcher staunchly resisted their proposals, settled on the EPG as a tool of diplomatic pressure. The group of Commonwealth elders comprised former Australian prime minister Malcolm Fraser, former military ruler of Nigeria General Olusegun Obasanjo, British banker Lord Barber, president of the World Council of Churches Dame Nita Barrow, former Tanzanian foreign minister John Malecela, former Indian Minister of External Affairs Sardar Swaran Singh, and primate of the Anglican Church in Canada, Archbishop Edward Scott.

The EPG visit was tolerated by the Botha administration, which was nevertheless clearly not interested in being pressured into talks; the EPG was still in the country when Pretoria ordered cross-border strikes on ANC targets in Harare, Lusaka and Gaborone, and the Commonwealth grandees went home disappointed and empty-handed.

Botha would almost certainly have been mindful of the mounting threat of right-wing disenchantment. Just four days after the EPG initiative had collapsed, a clash in the Transvaal town of Pietersburg seemed to hint at the potential of a new front of violence. The hard-right AWB had vowed to stop Foreign minister Pik Botha from addressing a Nationalist event to mark the centenary of the old Boer republic town. It was a 'battle of the burghers', one newspaper said, the Jack Botes Hall clouded in tear gas fired by police after AWB members overran the stage. Local and world television audiences were treated to the rare sight of

---

18 March Israel freezes military contracts and imposes cultural and tourism sanctions on South Africa.
22 March Archbishop Tutu meets the ANC in Zambia and fails to convince the organisation to abandon the armed struggle.

May South African agents attack ANC offices and safe houses in Maputo and Harare.
6 May National Party wins general election, but the rightwing Conservative Party replaces the PFP as official opposition.
11 June State of emergency renewed.

9 July Margo Commission of Inquiry into the death of President Samora Machel blames pilot error and negligence for the crash, discounting Soviet and Mozambican claims that the plane was lured off course by a decoy radio beacon.

panicking Afrikaners fleeing after bloody brawls, and a white policeman running from eye-stinging tear gas. The Pietersburg fracas was a sideshow, though, to the deathly cycle of violence in the townships, a low-level civil war which the state of emergency did little to stem, and probably only inflamed.

It had become obvious that there was little the government could do to appease black anger or strengthen the argument of moderates. Reforms of 1986 included repealing the Influx Control Act, granting freehold property rights in townships and opening central business districts of major towns and cities to trading by people of all races, but these were too little, too late. Sustained repression was the overriding strategy. More than 8 000 people were detained after the limited state of emergency in 1985, and this figure more than trebled in the year from June 1986 when a further 26 000 were taken in by police.

Monitoring events from his Pollsmoor cell, prisoner 466/64 sensed in the weeks after the EPG's failure and the start of the new state of emergency that while a discussion about negotiations might have seemed 'inauspicious', it was also true that 'often the most discouraging moments are precisely the time to launch an initiative', since that is when 'people are searching for a way out of their dilemma'.

Mandela asked for a meeting with the commissioner of prisons 'on a matter of national importance' and, when he met him some days later, said he wanted to meet Justice minister Coetsee. Remarkably enough – on reflection, Mandela sensed the Nationalists were anticipating a meeting – a rendezvous was arranged immediately. Still in his prison clothes, the ANC leader was driven to Coetsee's suburban residence where, settled on comfortable chairs in his lounge, the two men spent three hours discussing the core obstacles to talks: the armed struggle, and future constitutional guarantees for minorities, whites particularly. And, Coetsee wanted to know, did Mandela represent the ANC?

Mandela was satisfied with this initial contact and was keen to have further meetings, especially with PW Botha himself. But days, weeks and months passed and he heard nothing. He wrote again to Coetsee, and though he did not receive a direct reply, it was clear something was afoot. Towards the end of December, to his usual prison routine were added regular excursions into the city and further afield, to familiarise him – he surmised – with a society that had changed

9 to 12 July More than 60 white South Africans, mainly Afrikaners, meet the ANC in Dakar.

30 July A bomb explodes outside the headquarters of the South African Defence Force, injuring soldiers and civilians.

7 September An intricate prisoner exchange takes place in Maputo, involving 133 Angolan soldiers, anti-apartheid activists, Dutch anthropologist Klaas de Jonge, French university lecturer Pierre André Albertini and Major Wynand du Toit, a South African officer captured in Angola two years earlier.

11 September Revised National Statutory Council, to provide a forum for blacks to discuss policy and assist in drawing up a new constitution, is proposed.

considerably since he last moved in it in the early 1960s. Contacts with Coetsee resumed in 1987.

If Mandela, and by extension the ANC, was the critical axis to which the government was compelled to align itself – but only in secret at this stage – parliamentary politics seemed to swing in the opposite direction. In the May 1987 general election, the bulk of white voters backed the repressive National Party with no less conviction (52% of the vote, giving the ruling party 133 seats), but there was a troubling sea change for the Botha administration as much as for its liberal opposition in the startling gains made by Andries Treurnicht's Conservative Party. The CP, with 27% of the vote (23 seats) overtook the Progressive Federal Party (20 seats), placing the government to the left of its official opposition for the first time since 1948.

Ultimately, it didn't matter a great deal – except in as much as it only emboldened opposition outside Parliament. Newly appointed Anglican Archbishop of Cape Town Desmond Tutu and fellow outspoken cleric, Dutch Reformed

Archbishop Desmond Tutu addresses a Mass Democratic Movement gathering at St George's Cathedral in Cape Town in the late 1980s at the start of a fresh campaign of defiance of apartheid laws.

24 September Congress of Traditional Leaders of South Africa is launched to articulate the interests of tribal chiefs and act as an extra-parliamentary opposition movement.

27 September Tambo denies the ANC is in contact with the government.

5 October Botha rejects scrapping of Separate Amenities Act, but agrees that some residential areas can be opened to all races.

12 October Wynand Malan, a former National Party MP, leads newly formed National Democratic Movement, which is to develop contacts with black politicians.

5 November Govan Mbeki is released from Robben Island after 23 years in prison.

Mission Church moderator Allan Boesak, warned of white South Africa's entering the political 'Dark Ages' in this election, and vowed to step up pressure on the international community to disinvest. 'It is our last chance of bringing about a resolution of the crisis,' Tutu said.

The steadily declining relevance of whites-only politics was deepened two months later when IDASA, under former MPs Van Zyl Slabbert and Boraine, took a group of more than 60 leading South Africans, most of them Afrikaners, to Dakar in Senegal to meet senior figures in the exiled ANC. The initiative, co-sponsored by France Libertés, a human rights organisation run by Danielle Mitterrand, wife of the French president, enraged PW Botha, who called the excursionists 'political terrorists'. But, to the criticism widely expressed in white society that IDASA had succeeded merely in giving credibility to an ANC bent on the violent overthrow of the state, Alex Boraine pointed out: 'The simple answer is,

1988

February Botha opens Parliament with a speech ignoring the country's domestic crisis.

24 February Seventeen anti-apartheid organistions are banned, among them the AZAPO and COSATU.

27 February AWB members march to Pretoria to call for a *volkstaat* for Afrikaners.

17 March Dennis Worrall, former ambassador to the United Kingdom, establishes the Independent Party.

3 April International Convention against Apartheid in Sports takes effect.

7 April Leading lawyer and ANC activist Albie Sachs is critically injured in a bomb explosion in Maputo.

of course, that we met with them because they have credibility, they have been in existence for 75 years and their real base of support is not in Lusaka or in London but in South Africa.'

The ANC, it was now obvious, was the largest single party in the country, yet was excluded on account of being banned. A telling footnote of the Dakar encounter, at which ANC information secretary Thabo Mbeki led the liberation movement delegation, appeared in one newspaper report of the opening session: 'Thabo Mbeki also spoke but he may not be quoted … because he is banned.'

The historic three-day conference in Senegal was by no means a chummy indaba. Van Zyl Slabbert characterised the debates as 'some of the toughest I have heard in a long time'. But he and members of the ANC delegation expressed deep satisfaction at the outcome and vowed to continue the contact and even broaden it. An unnamed senior ANC member told an international press conference at the end of the meeting: 'All those who have been here in the past three days are changed persons. It has reaffirmed our earlier belief that Afrikaners and Africans can and will resolve the conflict in South Africa.'

And this, simply enough, was the essence, or at least the potential, of the first meeting – at the officers' club at Pollsmoor prison – between Nelson Mandela and a 'secret working group' of senior government officials in May 1988. It sprang from his earlier discussions with Justice minister Coetsee, contacts of which, by now, Mandela's prison colleagues and Oliver Tambo in Lusaka had been made aware.

The primary difficulty to emerge in the weeks and months of exchanges that followed was, in sum, the National Party's lack of confidence in its ability to convince whites to back genuine change after having repeatedly vowed it would never negotiate with any organisation committed to violent opposition. The ANC, his interlocutors kept telling Mandela, had to renounce violence. He in turn kept pointing out that the violence originated in government repression and apartheid itself. When at last the government's working group put it to him that in order for talks to begin the ANC would have to offer a compromise so that the Nationalists would not lose face with their own people, Mandela acknowledged that it was a 'fair point', one he could understand, but that 'it is not my job to resolve your dilemma for you'. He told them they 'must tell their people that

ANC and Afrikaner participants (opposite page, top) met for talks in Dakar, Senegal, in July 1987. Delegation leaders Frederik van Zyl Slabbert of the Institute for a Democratic Alternative in South Africa (IDASA) and Thabo Mbeki, the ANC's information secretary, flank their host, Senegalese President Abdou Diouf (opposite page, below).

19 April General Jannie Geldenhuys, Chief of the South African Defence Force, reveals details of South African military operations, codenamed Modular and Hooper, directed against SWAPO forces in Angola.

21 April Botha outlines reform plans, involving a form of race federation and draft legislation providing for new regional assemblies for blacks living outside the existing 'homelands'. He is warned that legitimate black leaders will reject them.

10 May International Commission of Jurists alleges widespread use of force and torture by security forces.
New Nation and *South* newspapers are banned; 26 editors hand petitions to government protesting against the curbs.

there could be no peace and no solution to the situation in South Africa without sitting down with the ANC. "People will understand," I said.'

Prolonged treatment for a lung condition at hospitals in the Cape Peninsula was followed by his being moved in December 1988 to a comfortable house in the grounds of Victor Verster prison in the winelands between Paarl and Franschhoek. Meaningfully, in the course of a now typically convivial visit, Coetsee told Mandela that this would be his last home before becoming a free man. It would take a little more than a year to reach that point.

A month later, in a memorandum to President Botha, whom he had yet to meet, Mandela put his finger on the primary stumbling block in the whole enterprise when he wrote: 'The truth is that the government is not yet ready … for the sharing of political power with blacks.' Nothing else mattered nearly as much – certainly not the government's enduring anxieties about the armed struggle or the linkage between the ANC and the South African Communist Party. And without facing up to it there was no hope of breaking the deadlock.

A mild stroke that January precluded Botha's participation in the historic beginnings of South Africa's rapprochement. In July, Mandela finally met Botha; having dreaded the meeting, he found his old foe 'unfailingly courteous, deferential and friendly' in a half-hour meeting that was 'friendly and breezy until the end'. He decided that while the encounter was 'not a breakthrough in terms of negotiations', it was in the sense that Botha, who had long talked about the need to cross the Rubicon, 'never did it himself until that morning at Tuynhuys'. Mandela took it as a sign that 'there was no turning back'.

More than anyone, Mandela was the author of the moment. One of his closest friends, fellow Rivonia trialist Ahmed Kathrada, had fiercely opposed his unilateral opening gambit with the Nationalists, but later acknowledged that it was 'the masterstroke of a visionary, and it changed everything'.

Months earlier, PW Botha's compromised health had prompted him to stand down as party leader while remaining State President, almost certainly a miscalculation that cost him the authority he presumably counted on retaining. The man who won the third round of the caucus ballot to become the new party leader was not held to be much of a reformist or a man who would, or even could, seriously challenge Botha.

Former President PW Botha speaks at a gathering of the faithful at the Voortrekker Monument in 1989. His successor FW de Klerk's 'new trek' was about to begin.

11 May Four white guerrillas, known as the Broederstroom Four, are arrested and an arms cache is discovered.
10 June State of emergency renewed.
16 June More than a million workers observe a stay-away on the 12th anniversary of the Soweto uprising.

21 June For the first time, the International Olympic Committee urges international sporting bodies to cut remaining ties with South Africa.
12 July The 'Sharpeville Six', sentenced to hang for the killing of a black local councillor, receive an indefinite stay of

execution to pursue a possible appeal. Botha grants them a reprieve on 23 November.
18 July On Nelson Mandela's birthday, the pro-government newspaper Beeld urges the government to release him.

3 August Eight Commonwealth foreign ministers press for a ban on coal imports from South Africa and on new loans to Pretoria.

14 August Mandela admitted to Tygerberg Hospital, suffering from a lung ailment.

18 August Botha rules out any possibility of a black majority government in South Africa.

31 August South African Council of Churches headquarters, Khotso House, is devastated by a bomb blast.

12 September Botha visits Mozambique and promises President Joaquim Chissano that South Africa will not support RENAMO. He also visits Malawi and Zaire, and, in October, meets Ivory Coast's President Félix Houphouët-Boigny.

FW de Klerk's public statements in the late Botha years – in favour of segregation, and against, among other things, black union rights and any softening towards the ANC – help to explain why his political impulses were so poorly judged in early 1989. One leading political commentator said confidently: 'He is likely to lead the party and the country along much the same lines as President Botha, with little major innovation.' This was not a controversial view.

Yet, as conditions in the country worsened, sanctions became more stifling, the rand dropped to new lows and pessimism deepened, the Nationalists realised that tricameralism was a failure and that the old man, the 'Groot Krokodil' (Great Crocodile) as he was not so affectionately nicknamed, was no longer up to leading South Africa out of its crisis. In De Klerk, they found an astute rationalist capable of weighing all options, even unthinkable ones, and making realistic choices.

PW Botha tried to hold on, but it was too late; his power had left him. Just a month after his 'friendly and breezy' meeting with Mandela, Botha appeared on national television in August 1989 to tell the country, bitterly, that 'after all these years of my best efforts for the National Party and for the government of this country, I am being ignored by ministers serving in my cabinet [and] I consequently have no choice but to announce my resignation.' He had mainly been ignored by the new party leader. De Klerk, who had already revealed his reformist inclinations, had taken the trouble to arrange a visit to Zambia to assure President Kenneth Kaunda of his sincerity, and win an ally – but without deferring to Botha beforehand.

The larger geopolitical setting was propitious. Soviet premier Mikhail Gorbachev's 1988 call for a 'new world order' had – along with superpower nuclear disarmament commitments – signalled the end of the Cold War. In the second half of 1989, the Iron Curtain was rendered diaphanous by the opening of the loathed Berlin Wall. Closer to home, following its defeat in the Angolan conflict, South Africa's agreeing to withdraw troops from South West Africa in exchange for the withdrawal of Cuban troops from Angola formed the basis of a negotiated solution which led to democratic elections in Namibia in 1989.

The fading of the Red threat, long exploited by apartheid South Africa to justify its total onslaught/total strategy schema, gave De Klerk more room to

16 October South African rugby officials meet ANC officials in Harare to discuss 'normalising' the sport and getting South Africa back into international competition.

1 November Government suspends the *Weekly Mail* newspaper for a month.

15 November Rightwinger Barend Hendrik Strydom massacres six blacks in a Pretoria street.

7 December Mandela is transferred to a house in the grounds of Victor Verster prison near Paarl.

22 December Angola, Cuba and South Africa end eight months of negotiations under US mediation for a settlement in South West Africa. The formal treaty is signed at the UN in New York.

The South African Defence Force's withdrawal from Namibia at the end of the 1980s paved the way for independence in the long-occupied territory and the election of a SWAPO government in Windhoek.

manoeuvre. Like East Europeans, though, South Africans were massing to demolish their old order too. Twelve days before Botha's rancorous resignation, a fresh popular assault on apartheid was launched by the Mass Democratic Movement, a new front to emerge as a result of restrictions on the UDF, COSATU and other political groupings.

Knowing that he did not have the luxury of time to plan at leisure, but, equally, that he would need whites broadly to endorse his thinking, De Klerk counted on gaining a reform mandate in the September general election – necessitated by

1989

5 January ANC agrees to close its military training bases in Angola; in return, South Africa must stop aid to the rebel Angolan UNITA movement.

12 January Researchers at the Indicator Project of South Africa state that unrest between September 1984 and June 1988 was the worst in South Africa's history, with more than 3 500 killed, and more than 55 000 imprisoned.

18 January Botha suffers a mild stroke.

2 February FW de Klerk takes over as National Party leader; Botha remains State President.

Botha's resignation – so that he could give his full attention to black demands. While the poll showed Nationalist support continuing to bleed away – the party lost 21 seats, with the anti-reform Conservative Party climbing in three years from 23 to 41 seats – the liberals, now regrouped as the Democratic Party, increased their share from 20 to 34 seats. Viewing the outcome in terms of sentiment for and against reform rather than merely support for the NP, De Klerk took the overall ballot as a clear endorsement, and pressed on. He displayed a new spirit of tolerance in removing restrictions on protests, allowing a mammoth march through central Cape Town that did much to convey his implicit willingness to engage. Weeks later, in October, he ordered the release of the remaining Rivonia prisoners and others, including Walter Sisulu, Ahmed Kathrada, Andrew Mlangeni, Raymond Mhlaba, Elias Motsoaledi, Jeff Masemola, Wilton Mkwayi and Oscar Mpetha.

In November, beaches were opened to all races and plans announced to scrap the Separate Amenities Act. Within government, De Klerk moved – as he later described it – 'to dismantle the powerful structures that the securocrats had developed under PW Botha'. (He acknowledged in the late 1990s that, not for want of trying, his success was limited.) Finally, in December, he met Nelson Mandela in the presidential suite at Tuynhuys, in Cape Town. The two men were mutually impressed, each concluding – in the approving idiom used by Margaret Thatcher after her first meeting with the Soviet reformer Gorbachev – that the other was a 'man we can do business with'.

The new Nationalist leader 'seemed to be making a real attempt to listen and understand', Mandela said of the encounter. 'I was able to write to our people in Lusaka that Mr De Klerk seemed to represent a true departure from the National Party politicians of the past.'

Few people had any inkling at the beginning of 1990 of the extent of De Klerk's imminent departure from the habitual conservatism of four decades of National Party rule. He recalled some years later how, moments before delivering his speech of 2 February, he had turned to his wife as they waited on the steps of Parliament and confided: 'After today South Africa will never again be the same.'

Six months earlier, the ANC and its partners in COSATU and the UDF had met in Zimbabwe to hammer out their minimum demands. The Harare Declaration called for a democratic non-racial state, negotiations on which could

---

4 February National Democratic Movement, Progressive Federal Party and Independent Party merge to form Democratic Party (DP).

16 February UDF and COSATU distance themselves from Winnie Mandela and her personal bodyguard.

21 March Power struggle between Botha and De Klerk ends in compromise; Botha will call an election later in the year.

1 May Wits academic and activist David Webster shot dead outside his home.

9 June Three-year-old state of emergency renewed for another year.

29 June National Party adopts five-year programme of reform aimed at giving blacks a role in national and local government affairs. The ANC says it will consider nothing less than one man, one vote.

Central Cape Town is packed with peace marchers in late 1989 in the first mass demonstration permitted by the government since the imposition of emergency regulations three years earlier. Among the march leaders was Archbishop Desmond Tutu, visible in his purple robes in the centre of the throng.

begin only once the government had unconditionally released all political detainees and prisoners, ended political trials, lifted bans on individuals and organisations, withdrawn troops from the townships, and ended the state of emergency.

As De Klerk began his speech on 2 February, central Cape Town was thronged with thousands of protesters chanting their support for these demands. By the end of the morning, the defiant shouts had turned to cheering and grinning disbelief; the government had, in effect, conceded the failure of white minority rule and come closer to meeting the Harare demands than anyone had imagined was even remotely conceivable.

5 July Mandela meets Botha; both confirm their 'support for peaceful development in South Africa'. In a separate statement released through the prison authorities, Mandela says only dialogue with the outlawed ANC will bring peace.

19 July De Klerk meets Mozambican president Joaquim Chissano.
2 August Mass Democratic Movement launches new campaign of defiance.
14 August Botha resigns as State President.

28 August De Klerk gains Zambian president Kenneth Kaunda's support in talks at Livingstone.
6 September National Party wins general election. De Klerk becomes President on 14 September.

His announcements took the exiled ANC completely by surprise: unbanning the African National Congress, the Pan Africanist Congress and the South African Communist Party; undertaking to free Nelson Mandela soon; lifting emergency restrictions on organisations such as the UDF and COSATU; releasing scores of political prisoners; lifting media restrictions; and declaring his government's commitment to creating a 'totally new and just dispensation' based on equality.

It was so unexpected, even out of character. De Klerk's saying the 'agenda is open' and the 'overall aims' included 'a new, democratic constitution' and a 'universal franchise' seemed convincing enough, with most in Lusaka and elsewhere seeing it as a genuine opportunity for open politics, but others at first suspected it might be a ruse. Their reaction reflected the decades of suspicion and mistrust born of the Nationalists' long indifference towards the black majority.

Perhaps the most optimistic voice was that of Thabo Mbeki. 'If Mr De Klerk says the time for talking has come,' the ANC's foreign affairs secretary said from Stockholm, 'we may be saying the same thing ourselves.' At home, Archbishop Desmond Tutu said De Klerk had 'taken my breath away'. Investors rewarded the President with an overnight boost on the Johannesburg Stock Exchange of R9 billion. In contrast to the international disdain of preceding years, congratulations poured in from the world, even from United Nations secretary general Xavier Perez de Cuellar.

It was all very dramatic. Jam-packed cars and taxis cruised city streets, hooters blaring, ANC flags fluttering from the windows. 'Our world,' Mandela later remarked, 'had changed overnight.' In a matter of hours the country had turned, and there was no going back. Conservatives were angry and anxious, but the bulk of whites, though many were apprehensive, seemed relieved by the bold, confident departure. A new South Africa, though it would take years to fashion, seemed possible at last.

Nelson Mandela and his wife, Winnie, raise
their fists in triumph on 11 February 1990
as the ANC leader takes his first steps to
freedom after 27 years behind bars.

15 October Seven jailed senior ANC leaders and Jafta Masemola of the PAC, convicted of sabotage in 1963, released from prison.

28 November De Klerk announces disbanding of National Security Management System, which had been introduced in 1979.

December All-inclusive black political conference in Zimbabwe adopts the Harare Declaration setting out preconditions for negotiations.

13 December De Klerk meets Mandela.

16 December Five anti-apartheid leaders, imprisoned in 1988 for political activities, are freed from Robben Island, including UDF general secretary Popo Molefe and publicity secretary Patrick Lekota.

1990

January Eight veteran ANC leaders, together with leaders of the Mass Democratic Movement and COSATU, meet the exiled ANC in Lusaka.

2 February De Klerk unbans the liberation movements, suspends the death sentence pending review, lifts restrictions and declares the government's willingness to engage in fundamental negotiations.

11 February Mandela freed after 27 years in jail.

27 February Mandela meets ANC officials in Lusaka.

Rivonia veterans, including Nelson Mandela's confidant Walter Sisulu (centre), at a welcome-home rally in Soweto on their release from prison in October 1989.

Central to it was Nelson Mandela, whose release a week later – at a time and in a fashion chosen by the prisoner – was, as the historian William Beinart cast it, 'a televised event of religious intensity – the raising of a man from another world who seemed to carry the promise of salvation'. Mandela himself, his 10 000 days of imprisonment over, felt at 71 that 'my life was beginning anew'.

Everybody was euphoric. But when, only hours after leaving his last prison home, Mandela addressed the thousands who filled Cape Town's Grand Parade – and a world audience of many millions – he left no doubt that the real achievements had yet to be made. While acknowledging De Klerk for having 'gone further than any other Nationalist President in taking real steps to normalise the situation', the ANC leader went on to say, almost ominously: 'The factors which necessitated the armed struggle still exist today. We have no option but to continue … Our struggle has reached a decisive moment. We call on our people to seize this moment so that a process towards democracy is rapid and

2 March ANC elects Mandela as its deputy president, and announces decision to move headquarters from Lusaka to Johannesburg as soon as possible.
20 March Namibia gains independence.

26 March Police kill 14 and injure more than 300 protesters at Sebokeng. In protest, on 31 March, the ANC calls off scheduled 11 April talks with the government.

March Minister of Education Piet Clase says white state schools may enrol black children from 1991 if most parents at the schools give their consent.
5 April Mandela and De Klerk agree to rescheduled talks in early May.

uninterrupted ... Now is the time to intensify the struggle on all fronts.' De Klerk was not alone in not thinking much of what seemed a belligerent party political speech – it was, in fact, the ANC's address more than Mandela's – but there was no doubting the authority, and the importance, of the freed man.

To begin with, a naive optimism informed speculation about the future – a new constitution by the end of the year, a black government soon thereafter. The opening three-day parley in Cape Town in May amounted chiefly, in the catch phrase of the time, to 'talks about talks'. The joint Groote Schuur Minute issued at the close focused on clearing obstacles to real negotiations, such as freeing political prisoners, granting immunity from prosecution to ANC members within and outside the country (at least 20 000 exiles awaited repatriation), lifting emergency regulations, and reviewing security legislation. It was a step forward, if a modest one.

In his signature urbane fashion, Thabo Mbeki told journalists: 'We were a bit surprised, I think, at how foolish all of us have been because in a matter of minutes everybody in the room understood that nobody there had horns.' That was doubtless true, but the mammoth task of 'normalising' politics – never mind society – was daunting. Wherever South Africans turned, they confronted real and abstract features of a once-fixed architecture of racialism and inequality that often risked upsetting the advance towards a new order.

And what was not properly foreseen in 1990 was just how violent the political contest would become, with every party to the talks – the liberals being the only exception – having their own arms and being quite willing to use them. The challenge of negotiating a future, and assuring their own stake in it, was thrust on organisations that were ill-prepared for it, but eager at every moment to assert their claims.

The apparent contradiction at the heart of the process – the ANC maintaining the armed struggle (in name, at least), the government being compelled to pull back its forces – was not squarely addressed until 6 August, when the two sides signed the Pretoria Minute, an agreement prompted by the ANC's unilateral decision to suspend the armed struggle. The government, in turn, committed itself to setting target dates for the release of political prisoners, and amnesty for crimes committed with political objectives.

Overleaf
Riot police confront demonstrators in Alexandra township, Johannesburg, when protests spiral after the stalling of the first round of CODESA talks in mid-1992.

14 April Mandela admits the ANC tortured dissident guerillas, but says officials involved had been punished and torture banned.

27 April ANC leaders Thabo Mbeki, Joe Slovo and others return to South Africa from exile.
2-4 May Groote Schuur talks between government and ANC deliver preliminary agreements on conditions for full-scale negotiations.

6 May Botha resigns from the National Party in protest against De Klerk's reform proposals.
7 May Indemnity Act provides exiles with temporary immunity or permanent indemnity against arrest or prosecution.

May De Klerk tours nine European countries.

May/June Mandela embarks on six-nation African tour, and 13-nation world tour.

8 June National state of emergency is lifted, except in Natal.

6 July ANC condemns 'tolerant attitude the South African authorities have adopted to the violent activities of far-right and fascist groups' after a bomb at a Johannesburg bus/taxi terminal injures 25. Extreme-right

'Wit Wolwe' (white wolves) group claims responsibility for five other bombings.

25 July Senior ANC member Mac Maharaj and over 40 other ANC and SACP members are detained for allegedly attempting to overthrow the government (Operation Vula).

7 **August** ANC's armed struggle suspended in terms of the Pretoria Minute. The government undertakes further reviews of security legislation 'to ensure free political activity'. Both sides commit to redoubling efforts to reduce violence.

16 **August** De Klerk and Mandela hold emergency meeting on violence, after Zulu migrant workers armed with axes and spears attack passengers at a Soweto train station. More than 500 die in 11 days of fighting between township residents and migrant Zulu workers in the PWV region; a state of emergency is imposed in this region.

1 **September** Justice Richard Goldstone's report on the Sebokeng killings criticises police for 'quite immoderate and disproportionate' action.

Bristling with 'cultural weapons', Inkatha-aligned hostel residents in Thokoza, Johannesburg, assemble in impi formation. Such a show of force was often a prelude to violence in what became known as the 'hostel war' of the negotiations era.

Two months earlier, De Klerk had lifted the state of emergency everywhere except in Natal, where violence was worsening. Bloodshed, though, would continue to strain the process to the very end. Talks were constantly interrupted by outbreaks of violence that claimed an average of more than ten lives a day, a higher death rate than in the 1980s.

There was, broadly, enough public generosity to sustain the optimism, and there were gestures to match it. The custodians of Afrikaans, for instance, announced in 1990 that the word list and spelling rules of the language would be amended to eliminate offensive words such as 'meid' and 'kaffer'. The National Party itself took the almost contradictory, but perfectly rational, decision in

14 September Mandela says after meeting De Klerk that the government is convinced of 'some hidden hand' in township violence.
20 September ANC and Inkatha Freedom Party (IFP) reveal they held high-level talks

in Durban to discuss ending violence in Natal and the townships on the Reef.
24 September Winnie Mandela is formally charged with kidnapping and assault, and will stand trial with seven others over

the December 1988 murder of Stompie Moeketsi.
15 October Reservation of Separate Amenities Act repealed.
18 October Natal state of emergency lifted.

October to allow all races to join its ranks (without them it would have had no future) and renamed itself the New National Party.

Yet, as De Klerk would discover, distrust ran deep. Whenever there was a crisis, he and Mandela would routinely be the ones to meet and resolve it. But their relationship became increasingly strained, chiefly over violence, with each leader doubting whether the other was doing enough to curb it.

ANC suspicions mounted over what soon came to be called 'third force' activity: underhand conduct by rogue elements in the army and the police who were dead set on sabotaging negotiations, or, at the very least, channelling arms to, and encouraging, Mango-suthu Buthelezi's Inkatha movement in its vicious contest with the ANC in Natal and on the Witwatersrand. Some Nationalists saw in Inkatha a powerful ally to counter the ANC, yet confirmation of secret government funding for training armed Inkatha units damaged the government's credibility. (Revelations to this effect in 1991 prompted De Klerk to demote Defence minister Magnus Malan and Law and Order minister Adriaan Vlok.)

Reinforcing the bonds of traditionalism, Inkatha Freedom Party leader Chief Mangosuthu Buthelezi (left) joins Zulu King Goodwill Zwelithini at a 1991 commemoration of the British defeat at Isandlwana in 1879.

In some instances, police openly sided with Inkatha 'impis'. The government's apparently expedient posture was underlined by regulations strictly banning the display of weaponry in public, but excluding 'cultural weapons' – such as the 'tribal' spears and knobkieries favoured by Inkatha fighters. De Klerk himself lent some credence to claims of 'third force' involvement when he speculated a few years later: 'The possibility cannot be discounted that … some elements in our security forces were reluctant to dismantle their clandestine capabilities or to abandon people that they had come to regard as their allies.'

19 October De Klerk's proposal to open the National Party to all South Africans is accepted by the last of four provincial party congresses.

13 November Harms Commission criticises army and police counterinsurgency units,

but has no evidence that police operated death squads. The activities of the Civil Cooperation Bureau (CCB) are severely criticised.

13 December Tambo returns to South Africa after 30 years in exile.

1991

9 January Black children enrolled at 205 out of 2 000 former white schools, where parents voted in favour of racial integration.

De Klerk, in turn, felt aggrieved by what he perceived as the ANC's duplicity. In mid-1990, police claimed they had uncovered a plot to foment revolution – Operation Vula – and arrested its key figures. Mandela insisted the President had been misled by police and that the operation was, in fact, 'moribund'. But De Klerk notes that a year later Mandela praised Operation Vula members and 'boasted' about its success in bringing combatants and arms into the country.

The apartheid and colonial past bequeathed a 'deadly brew' to the negotiation era, as journalist Rich Mkhondo conceived of it:

> *Millions of blacks are caught in a spiral of landlessness, homelessness, unemployment and poverty. Add to that a clash between modern political structures and traditional tribal ones. Mix in a struggle for hegemony in the region between major political players. Stir in the security forces in all their guises … Add faceless, apparently trained killers such as the 'third force' … Sprinkle all that with ancient and recent political and social grudges, and you get a deadly brew.*

Two summit meetings between Mandela and Buthelezi in the first months of 1991 made little impact on the rising death toll among their supporters. Not even the signing of the National Peace Accord in September, by no fewer than 24 parties and organisations, was especially influential. The government's efforts to prove its sincerity in neutralising state-linked violence included two judicial commissions (under judges Louis Harms and Richard Goldstone) and purges of senior police and military officers. These measures helped reveal the extent of 'dirty tricks' and death squads, but without stamping them out entirely. 'We failed at that stage,' De Klerk later admitted, 'to get to the root of the totally unacceptable covert activities in which some elements of the security forces were involved.'

But the 'process' continued, nevertheless. Thousands of prisoners were freed from early in the year and the granting of immunity from prosecution to exiles was begun. White MPs in Parliament passed laws scrapping apartheid's keystone statutes – the Population Registration Act and the Group Areas Act – and modifying heaps of laws and regulations, on everything from marriage and merchant shipping to unemployment insurance and national parks, to expunge ubiquitous traces of racism.

---

29 January Mandela and IFP leader Mangosuthu Buthelezi meet in Durban and issue a statement on a joint peace strategy.

1 February De Klerk tells Parliament that the Land Act, Group Areas Act and Population Registration Act will be scrapped.

12 February DF Malan Accord between the government and the ANC reaffirms the right to peaceful protest and that ANC guerrillas will not be harassed. The ANC agrees not to recruit and train new MK members.

4 March UDF announces it will formally dissolve itself later in the year.

2 May De Klerk announces plans to revise some provisions of the Internal Security Act, and offers to include black opposition leaders in the Cabinet.

In July, the ANC held its first national conference in South Africa since its banning in 1960. There was an atmosphere of expectation and impatience. Demands for 'no compromise' and an mediate dismantling of white political power reflected mounting popular intolerance of delays. Sentiment was inflamed, too, by perpetual suspicion that the government was feeding conflict.

The ANC, no less than the government, was under pressure to deliver, and their working groups strove to clarify a process, efforts that were rewarded in the closing weeks of the year with the launch of talks, to be known as CODESA (Convention for a Democratic South Africa). Most, but not all, parties signed the Declaration of Intent (22 December), committing to a multiparty democracy in a unitary state; the Inkatha Freedom Party withdrew when extra delegations for the Zulu king and the KwaZulu administration were refused; the PAC opted out, believing the talks would only deliver a cosy deal between the two main parties; and the Conservatives refused to play ball until the principle of a white homeland was acknowledged.

Multiparty negotiations on the post-apartheid state begin at the Convention for a Democratic South Africa (CODESA) in Johannesburg on 21 December 1991.

May Ban on 'cultural weapons' excludes 'at this stage, spears' in townships that are declared 'unrest areas'.
June Key Union and apartheid laws, including the Land Act, Population Registration Act and Group Areas Act, are scrapped.

Internal Security Act is amended to disallow detention without trial and the banning of people or organisations. Promoting communism is allowed for the first time since 1950.

2 July ANC holds its first national conference in South Africa in 30 years, in Durban. Cyril Ramaphosa elected as secretary general, Mandela as president and Walter Sisulu as deputy president.

But despite a blistering public row, over violence and the retention arms, between Mandela and De Klerk on the first day of the CODESA talks, it was a start. Five working groups began work on principles for a new constitution, arrangements for an interim government, the future of the homelands, and setting target dates for the transition to democracy.

South Africa began 1992 in a more positive frame of mind, even if the resistance of some remained dogged. The significance of right-wing opposition was probably always overestimated, but so long as the central premise of apartheid – minority rule – remained in place, white conservatism had an artificial and perhaps even dangerous advantage. Thus, the February 1992 Nationalist by-election

July International Olympic Committee readmits South Africa as a full member 21 years after its exclusion. International Cricket Council grants full membership to the United Cricket Board of South Africa, allowing South African players to participate in Test matches by the end of 1991. The US

lifts certain sanctions against South Africa. Switzerland lifts 1974 limits on export of capital to South Africa, and Israel lifts 1987 sanctions, though a ban on new military contracts remains.

21 July Government admits funding Inkatha and its associated trade union, the United Workers Union of South Africa.
29 July De Klerk demotes Defence minister Magnus Malan and Police minister Adriaan Vlok over the cash-for-Inkatha revelations.

CODESA brought together all the parties in the negotiation process. On the opposite page, chief ANC negotiator Cyril Ramaphosa is shown conferring with Nelson Mandela at the start of the talks. The South African Communist Party's chief negotiators (left, above) were, from left, Raymond Mhlaba, Chris Hani and Joe Slovo. National Party leader President FW de Klerk (left, below) is flanked by Constitutional minister Gerrit Viljoen, left, and Foreign minister Pik Botha. Ramaphosa and Nationalist negotiator Roelf Meyer (above) emerged as the key deal-makers.

defeat in Potchefstroom, a safe seat since 1948, strengthened unignorable Conservative demands for an election to test white opinion on the direction the government was taking.

De Klerk's masterstroke was to call not an election but a referendum, which would pit the Conservatives against the rest. White voters were asked to say 'yes' or 'no' to the question, 'Do you support the continuation of the reform process which the State President began on 2 February 1990 and which is aimed at a new constitution through negotiation?' The ANC, recognising that a 'no' vote would be disastrous for its own ambitions as much as for the prospects of a negotiated settlement, set aside its considerable reservations about endorsing a racially

August Umkhonto we Sizwe holds its first conference in South Africa after 30 years.
9 August Bloody confrontation between the AWB and police at Ventersdorp.

11 August Ismael Mahomed becomes first 'black' judge appointed to the Supreme Court.
14 September National Peace accord signed by more than 20 political parties and organisations including the ANC, IFP and

a number of political parties, trade unions, religious and civic organisations, as well as the government.
18 September 24 policemen are suspended and will face charges from assault to murder for their role in township violence.

Tension runs high as police fire on ANC protesters – killing one man – three days after the June 1992 massacre of 24 men, women and children at Boipatong.

exclusive poll to urge whites to vote for talks. Traditional NP opponents on the left of the government, along with big business (which was anxious to relieve economic pressure), had no difficulty in siding with De Klerk.

The 17 March result was a resounding 68.7% endorsement of a negotiated future. With grim prescience, however, the BBC's southern Africa correspondent, John Harrison, voiced the fears of many when he told British viewers that violence 'is built into the political system of this country, and I think we will see continuing violence in the townships where black groups are competing for political control, and I think also we will see a backlash from the hard right.' For all the swelling pride that most South Africans felt at their return to the Olympic family at the Barcelona Games in July, political unanimity was elusive. The second round of CODESA in May foundered over apparently irresolvable differences on majority rule, power sharing – central to Nationalist ambitions – and the extent of regional or provincial powers.

8 November South African cricket team arrives in Calcutta for three one-day matches against India, South Africa's first international cricket contact since 1970.

30 November A two-day preparatory meeting clears the way for the Convention for a Democratic South Africa (CODESA).

December SACP holds its first legal congress in the country; Chris Hani replaces Joe Slovo as secretary-general.

Frustration in the ANC and among its allies prompted a 'rolling mass action' campaign to force the government's hand. Not for the last time, yet more sickening violence ensued. On 18 June, 46 men, women and children at an informal settlement at Boipatong were massacred by Inkatha supporters from a nearby hostel. In September, as ANC protests turned to the 'puppet regimes' of the anachronistic homelands, Ciskei soldiers killed 29 ANC demonstrators following a reckless charge on the homeland leader Brigadier Oupa Gqozo's forces in his 'capital' at Bisho.

Such incidents sapped national confidence, but the principals always managed to hold the course. After a hastily arranged summit, Mandela and De Klerk ordered their teams back to work. It was a collective endeavour, but indispensable to the process was a solid working relationship between two very different men, the 'most unlikely Tweedledum and Tweedledee of negotiations', as a journalist described them: the no-nonsense former mineworkers' leader Cyril Ramaphosa, the ANC's chief negotiator, and his Nationalist counterpart, the slighter, fresh-faced Roelf Meyer. The Nationalist negotiator once said of their 'good working relationship' that 'we could say not only that we could resolve problems, but that there was not a problem we could not resolve.'

This was certainly true of their marathon effort in September 1992 in rescuing the talks process by fashioning a Record of Understanding, which, early in the new year, led to the first sitting of the Multi-Party Negotiating Forum, replacing CODESA.

The outsiders would be the spoilers, or would try to be. After an 11-month hiatus, all of 26 parties resumed talks at the World Trade Centre in Kempton Park, Johannesburg, and the outlook for 1993 brightened. A tragic killing on the morning of Saturday 10 April might have reversed the gains had it not been for the astute leadership and authority of Mandela. The dead man was the widely respected and much-admired former MK commander and South African Communist Party general secretary Chris Hani, gunned down in his Boksburg driveway on his return from buying the newspapers at his local shop. The assassin was Polish immigrant Janusz Walus, his abetter a senior Conservative Party member, Clive Derby-Lewis. Both were soon arrested (and convicted and jailed in due course). South Africa seemed to be back at

13 December UN calls on international community to resume academic, scientific and cultural links with democratic anti-apartheid organisations and sporting links with unified non-racial sporting organisations, as well as to review existing restrictive measures.

20 & 21 December First meeting of CODESA; 17 of the 19 parties attending sign a Declaration of Intent, committing themselves to multiparty politics.

1992
22 January De Klerk and Mandela awarded the UNESCO Peace Prize.
27 January European Community formally lifts economic sanctions.

The far-right Afrikaner Weerstandsbeweging (AWB), led by Eugène Terre'blanche (centre, with grey beard), was scrupulous throughout the negotiations in displaying indignation and contempt, but failed to engage serious political attention.

the abyss; mob violence resumed, deaths mounted, shares slumped. But while talks were suspended briefly, Mandela's appeal for calm cooled the rage and enabled negotiators to return to the table.

A less worrisome – almost comic – flashpoint occurred in June when the AWB, along with a new umbrella grouping, the Afrikaner Volksfront (Afrikaner People's Front), stormed the talks venue at the World Trade Centre, smashing computers and daubing slogans on the walls.

The same could not be said of the series of attacks on civilian targets by the PAC's armed wing, the Azanian People's Liberation Army (APLA), culminating in the horrific grenade and rifle assault on the congregation of the St James Church in suburban Cape Town during their Sunday evening service in July. (The PAC, which abandoned its armed struggle only in 1994, condemned the attacks at the time, though APLA operatives were later granted amnesty for the St James Church massacre.)

20 February De Klerk announces referendum for whites to determine their support for the reform process.
6 March Black Sash's Repression Monitoring Group estimates 11 000 people have been killed in political violence since 1986.

18 March Resounding 68.7% 'yes' vote among whites endorses negotiations.
13 April Mandela announces his separation from Winnie Mandela citing 'differences on a number of issues' and 'circumstances beyond (their) control'.

21 April Five white Democratic Party MPs defect to the ANC.
12 May CODESA working group agrees on forming multiparty Transitional Executive Council, which can take decisions by an 80% majority.

There remained, however, a pervasive sense that a different, better future could be reached through talks. In the very month of the St James Church horror, the Multi-Party Negotiating Forum set 27 April 1994 as the date for the country's first democratic election. ANC/SACP negotiator Joe Slovo's compromise proposal to allow for a government of national unity until 2000, and job security for existing government employees for ten years, boosted confidence in the process and the prospects of a settlement.

In the marketplace and the media, the images and discourses of negotiation and compromise subtly promoted what historian William Beinart called 'a more inclusive South African identity'. At Mandela's advising, the UN lifted remaining

Chris Hani, the former MK commander and senior South African Communist Party member, who inspired loyalty and admiration from subordinates and peers, survived the struggle only to be assassinated in the final year of negotiations.

16 May CODESA talks deadlock; ANC threatens mass action if the government does not compromise on constitutional issues.

27 May Justice Richard Goldstone says his commission has received no evidence yet of a 'third force', but denounces the government for failing to 'take sufficiently firm steps to prevent criminal conduct by members of the security forces and the police', and accuses ANC and IFP for 'resorting to violence and intimidation in their attempts to gain control over geographic areas'.

16 June ANC protest campaign launched to back demands for an interim government and an elected assembly to write a new constitution.

17 June Boipatong massacre; ANC suspends bilateral talks with the government.

sanctions, as did the United States. International investors, encouraged by the announcement of an election date, showed renewed interest. The gold price recovered, and growth returned to a positive 1.2%. Business, labour and government put their heads together in the newly formed National Economic Forum to seek consensus on redevelopment and growth. International recognition of the transition-in-progress was affirmed in October when Mandela and De Klerk were jointly awarded the Nobel Peace Prize.

All the while, the talks continued intensively. Finally, in the early hours of 18 November, the 158-page founding document of democracy was approved by bleary-eyed negotiators, ushering in an all-party Transitional Executive Council under an interim constitution, rubber-stamped by the tricameral Parliament at its penultimate sitting on 22 November.

The changeover was remarkable for its constitutional seamlessness, as historian Robert Ross noted when he wrote that 'this meant that the transition from apartheid to democracy was achieved with constitutional continuity ... The country's laws might be changed; the supremacy of its law maintained.' In the years of talks, the NP had given up its demand for special minority rights and its opposition to an elected constituent assembly (to write the final constitution), while the ANC had embraced private property and a free-market economy – and both had carried their supporters with them.

*   *   *

The last haul was tense, but the momentum was compelling. In the months and weeks leading up to 27 April, recalcitrant homeland administrations came into the fold. Right-wing Afrikaners joined, too, behind former South African Defence Force chief General Constand Viljoen, whose breakaway Freedom Front won a concession that, if there was 'substantial support' for it, future negotiations could be held on a white 'volkstaat', or homeland.

At the last minute, Buthelezi's Inkatha Freedom Party came in from the cold on the strength of hastily negotiated terms – recognition of the kingdom of KwaZulu, and the protection of the institution of the Zulu monarch, his status and his constitutional role. Stickers bearing the party's name, logo and leader's picture had to be stuck on the 80 million ballot papers printed already.

14 July De Klerk disbands security force units, 31 and 32 Battalions, and controversial police unit Koevoet.
30 July UN special envoy Cyrus Vance brokers talks between ANC and government.

21 August ANC and government chief negotiators Cyril Ramaphosa and Roelf Meyer discuss resumption of negotiations; after De Klerk and Mandela meet on 26 August, both sides agree to resume talks.

7 September ANC march against the Ciskei government at Bisho ends in bloodshed.
October ANC releases report on inhumane treatment of inmates at its detention camps in Angola, Tanzania and Uganda.

With a staff of some 200 000, the Independent Electoral Commission (IEC) under Judge Johann Kriegler mounted in four months election preparations he had been told would be impossible to pull off in less than a year. The IEC's optimistic slogan, 'You're ready, we're ready, let's do it,' seemed, at times, rash.

But not even a last-gasp bombing campaign by rightists on the eve of the election could delay the historic moment. Some 20 blasts were set off, but the national resolve was unshakeable, a defiantly confident spirit captured by Archbishop Tutu when he told a special election service at St George's Cathedral in Cape Town: 'We are going to vote, and the elections are going to be free and fair, and so there to all those ghastly creatures who are trying to subvert us.'

The long, patient queues, curiously silent after the years of clamour and rage, dispelled any doubt about the democratic convictions of South Africa's more than 22 million voters. For all the problems – delays, ballot papers running out, even a strike for more pay by vote counters – the result, announced on 6 May, was declared 'substantially free and fair'. The ballot delivered a new 400-seat

Throughout the country, the long, patient queues on 27 April 1994 testified to the democratic resolve of millions of first-time voters.

---

26 November De Klerk proposes timetable for transitional process, envisaging fully representative government by 1994.
19 December De Klerk announces suspension or dismissal of 23 senior SADF officers.

1993

March Multiparty negotiations conference announces new talks forum.
24 March De Klerk reveals to special joint session of Parliament details of South Africa's past nuclear programme.

1 April 26 parties and organisations resume talks in Multi-Party Negotiatiing Forum.
10 April Chris Hani assassinated.
24 April Tambo dies.

Parliament that was very different from any before it; on 9 May, when Mandela was officially sworn in as an MP, the composed solemnity of old parliamentary ways was injected with a dose of vernacular liveliness in the form of Tembu *imbongi* (praise singer) Sthembile Mlangeni's strident paean to the new leader.

The ANC emerged, as expected, as the dominant force, winning 252 seats from its 62.5% share of the vote. The New National Party was next (82 seats, 20.4%), followed by the Inkatha Freedom Party (43 seats, 10.5%), the Freedom Front (9 seats, 2.2%), the Democratic Party (7 seats, 1.73%), the Pan Africanist Congress (5 seats, 1.25%), and the African Christian Democratic Party (2 seats, 0.5%). What had once been ruled out as unthinkable and impossible was, in the event, quite ordinary – though, of course, it had taken an extraordinary effort to achieve.

South Africa soon rejoined the Commonwealth after an absence of more than 30 years, took its place at the United Nations, which it had left in opprobrium 20 years before, became the 53rd member of the Organisation of African Unity, and joined the Non-Aligned Movement. Billions of rands were pledged in aid, diplomatic relations widened dramatically, and luminaries – the Queen, the Pope and the Dalai Lama, umpteen presidents and even Mother Teresa – flew in to wish the country well.

The challenges were titanic, a legacy of deep-set inequality, poverty and mistrust in a 'deeply divided society whose integrity,' historian David Welsh said at the time, 'will have to be ensured by the real, if fragile, bonds of interdependence and a sense of shared fate.' It meant that, in the next few years, South Africans would have to confront both their future and their past.

Yet further intensive negotiation ensued in the Constituent Assembly to produce the 1996 Constitution and Bill of Rights, which, in plain language, created the basis of a constitutional state founded on individual freedoms and rights, qualified by exceptions to match redress (such as race-based affirmative action), and a Constitutional Court as the final arbiter of the law.

In 1996, with the establishment of the Truth and Reconciliation Commission (TRC), the country began to confront the rot of its inescapable past, the reliance of succeeding apartheid administrations on abusing human rights to sustain their own survival, and white privilege as a whole, as well as the moral

7 May Of the 26 parties in the Multi-Party Negotiating Forum, 23 adopt a Declaration of Intent; in June, they set 27 April 1994 as the date for the first democratic election.
June Mandela and Buthelezi pledge to work together to curb violence.

26 June Right-wing assault on World Trade Centre, Kempton Park, the venue for the Multi-Party Negotiating Forum.
23 September Parliament passes new law to establish the Transitional Executive Council, to ensure free and fair elections.

24 September Mandela addresses the UN Special Committee against Apartheid, calling for the lifting of all economic sanctions against South Africa.
15 October De Klerk and Mandela are jointly awarded the Nobel Peace Prize.

errors of the liberation cause. (A 1992 Amnesty International report on the abuse, torture and execution of prisoners in ANC camps in Angola, Tanzania, Uganda and Zambia during the 1980s noted that 'this pattern of gross abuse was allowed to go on unchecked for many years, not only by the ANC's leadership in exile, but also by the governments of the Frontline states'. The ANC did set up its own commissions – the first in 1984, and two others, both in 1992 – to investigate abuses at its camps, particularly the notorious Quatro camp in Angola.)

It was clear, once the TRC began its emotionally draining and politically taxing work, that the overwhelming burden of guilt lay with apartheid for atrocities and abuse, negligence, brutality and moral failure welling from a system that was corrupt at its heart. It was a system which, especially in its late term, incorporated and counted on unexplained murders, corrupt relationships with international criminals, mysterious foreign bank accounts, vast sums spent on sponsoring violence and conflict in neighbouring states, multi-million-rand secret funds and fraudulent cash-hungry front companies, and death squads that were responsible for appalling atrocities.

After seven years, the R70 million TRC process came to an end in 2003 with the tabling in Parliament of the last of several volumes encompassing more than 21 000 victim statements arising from some 38 000 incidents and the killing of 14 000 people. The Amnesty Committee received 7 127 applications for amnesty, of which only 1 146 were granted.

Ironically, both the ANC and the National Party went to court to try to stop publication of sections of the report that reflected badly on them. The ANC's eleventh-hour intervention prompted Archbishop Tutu's fierce reaction: 'I have struggled against tyranny. I didn't do that in order to substitute another, and I believe if there is tyranny and an abuse of power then let them know that I will oppose it with every fibre of my being.'

If the exercise was unfinished and imperfect – it was necessarily part and parcel of the overriding objective of reconciling South Africans – it succeeded in embedding the idea that human rights is the indispensable condition of justice and democracy, and that truth, however hard it might be to acknowledge, is at once necessary and redemptive.

28 November Afrikaner Broederbond opens membership to women and all races, provided they speak Afrikaans.
6 December Transitional Executive Council begins its work.

1994
16 January PAC suspends armed struggle.
12 February 19 parties register for the April election.

16 February Mandela announces six concessions, including allowing provinces to determine their own form of government.
17 February Independent Electoral Commission hires 10 300 observers to monitor the first democratic election.

All this was still to come when Nelson Mandela delivered his inaugural speech as the first President of a democratic South Africa on 10 May 1994, a suitably stirring performance with its ringing cadences and indigenous colouring: 'I have no hesitation in saying that each one of us is as intimately attached to the soil of this beautiful country as are the famous jacaranda trees of Pretoria and the mimosa trees of the bushveld.'

'Today,' he said, 'all of us ... confer glory and hope to new-born liberty. Out of the experience of an extraordinary human disaster that lasted too long, must be born a society of which all humanity will be proud.' Few sentiments could have been truer than his acknowledgement – an echo of his self-defining declaration back in the 1960s – that 'there is no easy road to freedom'. But it was not a time for cheerlessness. 'Let freedom reign,' he told the ecstatic thousands. 'The sun shall never set on so glorious a human achievement!'

One among the crowd on the terraces below was a 17-year-old Afrikaner school-boy from Pretoria who, dressed in denim jeans and a 'Peace in SA' T-shirt with the new flag on it, had left home at sunrise to be sure not to miss anything. He was not an especially remarkable witness to Mandela's inauguration, but he retains a mod-est place in the record on the strength of a newspaper report which presented him as a member of that new class of citizen, an outwardly uncomplicated patriot. The headline over the story about Johann Grobler – 'Schoolboy Johann defies doom predictions to join in the fun' – describes the lingering apprehension among the beneficiaries of apartheid about a future that was perhaps too hard to grasp, as well as an unmistakable lightheartedness stimulated by the understandable if deceptive atmosphere of festivity. 'Everybody told me I was crazy,' Grobler was quoted as saying. 'They said I was going to die.' But all he wanted to do, this 'lone white face in a crowd of thousands', was join in the toyi-toying and singing. 'It's a great day in history,' he said finally, 'it's history in the making.'

The euphoria was real enough, the historic moment almost uncanny. If the undoubted sentimentality faded in time, and the hard grind of dealing with the tenacious legacy of the past would test South Africans' courage and convictions for years to come, 10 May 1994 marked the incontestable relegation of four and a half decades of apartheid as a formal system of constructed racial oppression. In that statutory sense at least, it was finally over, gone for good.

In a gesture at once of triumph and unity, Nelson Mandela joins hands with deputy presidents FW de Klerk and Thabo Mbeki at the presidential inauguration on 10 May 1994.

4 March General Constand Viljoen registers a new party, the Freedom Front, for the April election.

19 April IFP agrees to contest election, following talks between De Klerk, Mandela and Buthelezi.

23 April Government, ANC and Freedom Front sign an agreement on a possible separate state for whites.

26 to 29 April 22 million voters participate in first democratic election.

6 May First democratic elections declared 'substantially free and fair'.

10 May Mandela is inaugurated as President.

24 May In his first state of the nation address in Parliament, Mandela commits South Africa to government based on the Universal Declaration of Human Rights.

Postscript

The preaching and practice of national, race or colour discrimination and contempt shall be a punishable crime.

The Freedom Charter, 1955

The times in which one only had to be a white person in order to have an identity of one's own now belong in the distant past.

Minister of the Interior, SL Muller, 1969

South Africa's past, it could be said, craves attention for its considerable explanatory power, and it is, doubtless, the primary source of what's to come. Yet it's likely that receding episodes remain imperfectly understood – familiar enough to seem explicable, yet vividly restless, and given to yielding more imaginative options than this or that orthodoxy might seem capable of tolerating.

A decade and a half after what was deceivingly referred to as the 'miracle' of South Africa's transition to democracy, the central argument of public life – what it means to be free of the limits, penalties and consequences of earlier constructions of national identity – is still as fervently contested as ever.

The actual transformation of society since 1994 – the end of white political supremacy by the assertion of individual rights, and the considerable material changes that have occurred as a result in public and private life – is often contrasted with a social setting in which skin colour is still closely aligned with poverty or wealth, opportunity and political persuasion.

Against this, the formal programme of 'transformation' – legislated race-based interventions to engineer equity – has raised a fundamental question: is it possible to use the racial categories of an unlamented past to create a more desirable non-racial future? Conversely, is it possible to overcome racialism, or advantage based on race, without reference to race itself? In office and factory, suburb and township, on sports fields, in schools and universities, in government itself, and even within political parties, the question of what to do about apartheid all these years after its acknowledged failure remains a paramount consideration.

Arguably, the most ironic consequence of apartheid's demise is the revival of its central precept: definition of identity by race. 'Never again …' people said, even as they voted in their millions for policies which would, inevitably, concentrate rather than render diffuse the racial distinctions that formed the foundation of the old state. How else, though, to expunge racialism than by racialism itself? It's a thesis many still hold to, but it's a constantly embattled one.

Scholar and former Robben Island prisoner Neville Alexander argued forcefully in a polemic of April 2011:

Suffice to say that fighting race with race is bad social science and even worse practical politics. Besides tackling the structural economic and social inequalities that we took over without much modification from the apartheid state, we have to do the hard work of exploring, researching and piloting alternative approaches to those based on the apartheid racial categories to counter the perpetuation of white and other social privilege. It is a fundamental theoretical and strategic error to try to do so by perpetuating racial identities in the nonsensical belief that this will not have any negative or destructive social consequences.

South Africa's Alcatraz – Robben Island – seemed almost benign in the early 1990s when Nelson Mandela and fellow former Rivonia trialists Dennis Goldberg, Andrew Mlangeni, Ahmed Kathrada, Walter Sisulu and Wilton Mkwayi returned to the bleak island prison their gaolers had hoped would break their spirit.

There is an argument that, not unlike the post-1910 period – when the Afrikaner became the political inheritor of Union but suffered decades of economic inferiority and blight – the post-apartheid term lifted barriers to asset-rich whites, expiated their 'sins' and legitimised the normality of their self-realisation while leaving the vast bulk of liberated black South Africans mired in the deficiencies and disadvantages of their apartheid-era fate. In such circumstances, some observers have warned, the ruling party of the early 21st century, like the white Afrikaner nationalists of the 1930s and 1940s, has seemed willing to develop a brand of nationalism that at once nurtures and exploits an insidious association between economic grievance and racial resentment among the majority.

Yet it's equally clear that even within the ANC dissenting elements hold the Congress tradition of defending the Freedom Charter's lynchpin precept that the country belongs to all who live in it. This was nowhere more tellingly illustrated than in early 2011 when a veteran Cabinet minister rounded on a senior government official, accusing him of Verwoerdian racism. The widely respected former Finance minister, Trevor Manuel, exploited his considerable struggle credentials as an activist of the United Democratic Front of the 1980s to launch his remarkably unrestrained public attack on Cabinet spokesman Jimmy Manyi over disparaging remarks the independent-minded official had made a year earlier about the 'oversupply' of coloureds in the Western Cape. The party itself, in what it possibly regarded as unfussy democratic fashion, sided with Manyi, while the union federation, COSATU, the ANC's key alliance partner, sided with Manuel. Followers were no doubt divided too.

But did the spat herald a race schism in the party or an abandonment of the principles of the Freedom Charter? Neither of these, probably. More like more of the same, the continuing struggle of South Africans in accommodating themselves – even by the time-honoured means of resisting it – to the unignorable 'common condition' described by Olive Schreiner a century ago, a 'condition of practical necessity which is daily and hourly forced upon us by the common needs of life ... the one path open to us.'

It did suggest that as South Africa headed towards its third decade of liberation insufficient seriousness was being brought to bear on the risks of perpetuating race consciousness. The spectacle of one senior ANC member accusing another of Verwoerdian racism had the effect of delineating a black/coloured divide Verwoerd himself might have recognised as something almost of his own making. Yet, for all the heat of the moment, it passed – or at least was absorbed in normal political processes.

If, in the years that followed 1994, South Africa did not altogether succeed in reinventing itself as a truly non-racial state, it certainly succeeded in reimagining itself as a freer, fairer country founded on inalienable individual rights, free speech and regular elections, with a Constitutional Court serving as the final arbiter of government action and social conduct.

The range of this trajectory might well depend on the avoidance of simplistic views of the past that lend themselves to demagoguery, or at least to those false certainties that tend to limit the reach of optimism. In 2010, historian Bill Nasson cautioned against undue historical certitude when he observed that 'even as we move ever further into post-apartheid history, scholars still do not have all the answers to what kind of country it has been, to say nothing of what it may become. The most difficult challenge, perhaps, may be finding the right questions.'

It may be that the conviction of the 1990s that 'never again' would this society succumb to racialism was premature, either because it was simply expecting too much of democratic elections, a Bill of Rights and a willingness to give national cohesion a go to overcome the legacy of division and inequity, or because racial identity would for the time being – or always, for that matter – be a profitable basis for acquiring and sustaining power, in defiance of the dangers so starkly illustrated in recent history.

When Schreiner wrote of the 'common South African condition through which no dividing line can be drawn' in the early 1900s, she foresaw at least a century of labour to bring into being 'this unity which must precede the production of anything great and beautiful by our people as a whole'. A century might have been enough had it not been for the radical disjuncture of apartheid and all it bequeathed to the country's early 21st-century society.

Yet, for all that, Schreiner's vision – and indeed, the vision of, among others, Luthuli, Paton, Mandela and Mbeki – of a people welded by circumstance and need, interdependent and indivisible, is every day affirmed. The notable – perhaps for being unremarkable – thing about the apartheid catastrophe is that, for all the depth of its impact and the reach of its legacy, it failed. Being a South African is more than a geographical concept or an administrative classification to determine which queue to join at foreign airports. If it is far from being a settled identity, it is an identity bound up in the continuing argument about belonging. The argument persists, for the sense of belonging persists too. It is certainly not the same as unity, or a common vision, or, even less, mutual affection. But it does suggest that apartheid came and went because its divisions and divisiveness were disarmed, ultimately, by a much longer history of inseparability.

Bibliography

Alexander, Neville. *An Ordinary Country* (University of Natal Press, 2002).

Alhadeff, Vic. *A Newspaper History of South Africa* (second edition, Don Nelson, 1985).

Beinart, William. *Twentieth-Century South Africa* (second edition, Oxford University Press, 2001).

Bunting, Brian. *The Rise of the South African Reich* (International Defence and Aid Fund for Southern Africa, 1986; first published by Penguin African Library, 1964).

Callinicos, Luli. *The World that Made Mandela* (STE Publishers, 2000).

De Klerk, FW. *The Last Trek, A New Beginning* (Macmillan, 1998).

Giliomee, Hermann & Mbenga, Bernard. *New History of South Africa* (Tafelberg, 2007).

Huddleston, Trevor. *Naught For Your Comfort* (Collins, 1956).

Joyce, Peter. *South Africa in the 20th Century* (Struik Publishers, 2000).

Keppel-Jones, Arthur. *When Smuts Goes* (second edition, Shuter & Shooter, 1950).

Lapping, Brian. *Apartheid, A History* (Grafton Books, 1986).

Maclennan, Ben. *Apartheid. The Lighter Side* (Chameleon Press, 1990).

Mandela, Nelson. *Long Walk to Freedom* (Macdonald Purnell, 1994).

Meredith, Martin. *Fischer's Choice, A Life of Bram Fischer* (Jonathan Ball Publishers, 2002).

Morris, Michael. *Every Step of the Way* (HSRC Press, 2004).

Morris, Michael. *Paging through History* (Jonathan Ball Publishers, 2007).

Nasson, Bill. 'Can an abnormal country ever have a normal history?' (inaugural lecture, Department of History, University of Stellenbosch, August 2010).

Ross, Robert. *A Concise History of South Africa* (Cambridge University Press, 1999).

Saunders, Christopher (consultant editor). *Reader's Digest Illustrated History of South Africa. The Real Story* (third edition, Reader's Digest Association, 1994).

Saunders, Christopher. *Historical Dictionary of South Africa* (second edition, Rowman & Littlefield, 1983).

Schreiner, Olive. *Thoughts on South Africa* (Ad. Donker, 1992; first published by T. Fisher Unwin, 1923).

Welsh, David. *The Rise and Fall of Apartheid* (Jonathan Ball Publishers, 2009).

Worden, Nigel. *The Making of Modern South Africa: Conquest, Segregation and Apartheid* (Juta & Co/Blackwell Publishers, 1994).

Wright, Harrison M. *The Burden of the Present: Liberal-Radical Controversy over Southern African History* (David Philip, 1977).

NEWSPAPER SOURCES

Beeld

Die Burger

Cape Argus

Cape Times

Rand Daily Mail

The Star

ONLINE SOURCES

South African History Online (http://www.sahistory.org.za)

Wikipedia

Index

PICTURE CREDITS

Africa Media Online: p93 (District Six Museum);
pp6, 17, 21, 26-7, 31, 38-9, 47, 49 above and
below, 50, 52-3, 54-5, 59, 60, 63 left and right, 70,
72, 73, 75, 76, 79, 96, 101, 106-7, 108-9, 114-5,
123, 128 (Drum Social Histories/Baileys African
History Archive); pp86 (David Goldblatt/South
Photographs); p81 above (Chris Ledochowski/
South Photographs); p155 (John Liebenberg/
South Photographs); pp123, 145, 164-5, 170, 173
(Greg Marinovich/South Photographs); p136 (Guy

Tillim/South Photographs); pp110-11, 126-7 (Gille
de Vlieg/South Photographs); pp124, 135, 137, 141,
153, 175, 179 (Paul Weinberg/South Photographs);
pp2-3, 4-5, 81 below, 158-9, 162-3, 165, 167, 168,
169 above left, 172 (Graeme Williams/South
Photographs); p33 left (Martin Gibbs); pp149, 157,
160 (Eric Miller); p138 (Cedric Nunn); pp57, 65,
90, 113, 121 (Museum Africa); p179 (Guy Stubbs).
Cape Argus: cover, Les Hammond. **Institute for
Democracy in Africa (IDASA):** p150. **Media 24:**

pp103, 118. **National Archives of South Africa
(NASA):** p78. **National Library:** pp68, 85, 131.
Natural Cultural History Museum: p29. **National
Archives and Records:** p98. **PictureNet:** pp42,
82-83, 169. **Rand Daily Mail:** p9 (cartoon by Denis
Santry, 23 August 1914), p133 (cartoon by Bob
Connolly, 1977); **Topfoto/Inpra:** pp33 right, 181.
Umteteli wa Bantu: p37 (cartoon by Gerry Norton
[Umboneli], 1953). **www.southafrica.info:** p62
(South African Airways Open).

ACKNOWLEDGEMENTS

The author wishes to acknowledge with gratitude the invaluable contributions of Ceri Prenter, Alfred LeMaitre, Peter Bosman, Marius Roux, Carin Lilienfeld and Ingeborg Pelser. Thanks also to Farieda Classen, Mary Lennox and Paul Wise. A special thanks to Sharon Sorour-Morris and Kate and Jack for their forbearance and encouragement.

© Published edition 2012
Reprinted in 2013
Jonathan Ball Publishers
(A division of Media24 Pty Ltd)

First published in 2012 in paperback by
JONATHAN BALL PUBLISHERS (PTY) LTD
PO Box 33977
Jeppestown
2043
Reg No 1950/038385/07

ISBN 978-1-920289-41-6

Editor: Alfred LeMaitre
Cover design: Marius Roux
Book design: Peter Bosman

Reproduction by Resolution Colour, Cape Town
Printed and bound by Star Standard Industries (Pte) Ltd, Singapore
Set in Arno Pro 11 on 14.5pt